Greater Works

A Compilation of Prayers For Everyday Life

Greater Works

A Compilation of Prayers For Everyday Life

Sonja Pinckney Rhodes
Shanell R. Burwell
Karen A. Middleton
Dana P. Richardson
Rev. Patricia W. Crawford
Sherri Pinckney Kinloch

Copyright © 2019 "Greater Works" by Sonja Pinckney Rhodes, Shanell R. Burwell, Karen A. Middleton, Dana P. Richardson, Rev. Patricia W. Crawford, and Sherri Pinckney Kinloch

All rights reserved

No part of this book may be reproduced, stored in or introduced into a retrieval system, or transmitted, in any form or by any means (electronic, mechanical, photocopying, recording, or otherwise) without prior written permission from the publisher.

ISBN: 9781693663147

Some of the scriptures in this book were taken from the King James Version - Bible in Public Domain; New International Version (NIV) Holy Bible, New International Version®, NIV® Copyright ©1973, 1978, 1984, 2011 by Biblica, Inc.® Used by permission; The ESV® Bible (The Holy Bible, English Standard Version®). ESV® Text Edition: 2016. Copyright © 2001 by Crossway, a publishing ministry of Good News Publishers. Used by permission; and NEW AMERICAN STANDARD BIBLE®, Copyright © (NASB) 1960,1962,1963,1968,1971,1972,1973,1975,1977,1995 by The Lockman Foundation. Used by permission.

For information on the content of this book, email booksbysonja@gmail.com

WrightStuf Consulting, LLC, Columbia, SC

Printed in the United States of America

Table of Contents

Ms. Sonja Pinckney Rhodes 1
    Wisdom 4
    God's Light 7
    Talk with Jesus 10
    Our Rock 12
    Refuge 15
    All Have Fallen Short 17
    Provider 20
    Stand 21
    Purpose 23
    Thanks 25
    Strength 28
    God be Glory 30
    At the Altar 33

Ms. Shanell R. Burwell 35
    Prayer Is Powerful 39
    Relationship 40
    Healing, The Promise of Restoration 41
    Release the Burden 42
    My Exodus 43
    My Love Letter 44
    The One Chosen By God 45
    Collection of Souls 47

Oh, Heavenly Father,	47
Thank You	48
Righteousness Through Faith	50
The Key to Discernment	52
Deaconess Karen A. Middleton	**53**
At the Altar	57
Free from Unrighteousness	60
Divine Protection	62
Unconditional Love	63
Purify Me	64
Blessings for My Enemies	65
Widows and Widowers	67
Prayer for Family	68
Peace	70
A Troubled Heart	71
My Daily Assignment	73
Anxiousness	74
Encouragement	75
The Loss of a Loved One	76
Strength in The Storm	78
Corporate Prayer	80
Give Thanks	82
Rev. Patricia W. Crawford	**83**
Prayer of Praise and Worship	87
Prayer For Salvation	89

- Good Success 91
- Direction 93
- Meet the Needs 95
- Protection 98
- Purpose 101
- God's Will... 104
- Healing 107
- Warfare 109

Mrs. Dana P. Richardson 111
- Ever-Present Help 114
- Calm My Fears... 116
- This one's personal! 118
- Dearly Beloved, We Gather Together 119
- Breath Prayer 121
- Help My Unbelief!... 122
- When Joy Comes 123
- While Others Are Calling...................................... 124
- Lord, Lift Me!.. 125
- Lord, Prepare Me 126

Mrs. Sherri Pinckney Kinloch 127
- Strength... 131
- Gratefulness 132
- Healing 133
- Mercy 134
- Marriage 135

Be Steadfast 136
Hope 137
Honor 138
Glory 139
Praise 140

Introduction

Greater Works is an awesome testimony of six valiant women of God from different backgrounds, experiences, and walks of life who accepted their call to share how God has transformed their lives. They have penned so graciously their witness of His mighty works. Through prayers that speak volumes of their journey, you will experience how God held, carried, covered, sustained, renewed, and restored them, with each page. You'll feel their strength and growth into the character of God. The personal witnessing of His goodness and His grace is resounding for others to be inspired, delivered, and set free by His marvelous, and miraculous works.

The unspoken determination impelled these women of God, Shanell Burwell, Rev. Patricia Crawford, Sherri Pinckney Kinloch, Karen Major-Middleton, Sonja Pinckney Rhodes, and Dana P. Richardson to be willing vessels outpouring as of living streams of flowing waters conveyed through the thunderous waves of dreams dared to dream, hurts they overcame, despairs turned into hope, and triumphant victories. They all attest to the pivotal aspects of their lives that once spiraled through rising currents that were strengthened through their persistent prayers, by trusting God to bring them through their journeys of how He brought them over, through and out. Their prayers testify to the great work God continues to do in their lives, as stated in John 14:12, *Verily, verily, I say unto you, He that believeth on me, the works that I do shall he do also; and greater works than these shall he do; because I go unto my Father.*

Ms. Sonja Pinckney Rhodes

Psalm 1:2-3 (KJV)
² But his delight is in the law of the LORD; and in his law doth he meditate day and night. ³ And he shall be like a tree planted by the rivers of water, that bringeth forth his fruit in his season; his leaf also shall not wither; and whatsoever he doeth shall prosper.

Ms. Sonja Pinckney Rhodes is the author of *From Pain to Purpose: A Bridge Over Troubled Waters*, published in 2019, a South Carolina Realtor for Coldwell Banker Residential Brokerage, and a Business Manager at the Medical University of South Carolina where she has 28 years of service. In addition, she is the advisor for the Young Adult Ministry, advisor for the Baptist Young

Women Ministry, and she teaches biblical principles as a Young Adult Sunday School teacher for ages 18 - 36 years old at Mt. Moriah Missionary Baptist Church. Sonja has recently accepted a volunteer position at My Sister's House, as an advocate for battered and abused women. Ms. Rhodes earned her Master's Degree in Business Management with a Minor in Human Resource Management at Strayer University in 2014. She is a native of Charleston, South Carolina; the proud mother of two sons, Jon Pinckney and Andre' Rhodes, mother-in-law of one admired daughter-in-law, Markita Pinckney and three beautiful grandchildren, Jon Pinckney, Jr., Ari Pinckney, and Nia Pinckney.

Inspiration

As I accepted the call as a prayer warrior for an international prayer line that holds an average of 1000 listeners for 15 minute segments, in my despair, I cried out to the Lord to fill me, speak in me, and to speak out of me, that I may know the needs of those listening for an answer, and He did. His Word says to call unto me, and I will answer thee (Jeremiah 33:3).

The Lord began to awaken me in the middle of the night with prayers flowing out of me like rivers of living water. I launched prayers with my phone's flashlight illuminating just enough to write at 3 a.m. and 4 a.m. for the prayer line to be a blessing, to touch a heart, to heal a wounded spirit, and to save someone from detrimental thoughts and actions. It was never me, but the Lord. I shared my experience with my Pastor, Byron L. Benton, and he answered, "If the Lord tells you to write, then you write. You don't know who needs those prayers or what woman can't pray for herself."

I sought the Lord deeper, and He birthed this awesome mission in my spirit that would bridge others to experience His glorious prayers of affirmation, confirmation, healing, and deliverance.

Wisdom

My son, pay attention to what I say; turn your ear to my words. Do not let them out of your sight, keep them within your heart; for they are life to those who find them and health to one's whole body.
Proverbs 4:20-22

You see, God gives us His wisdom through His Word. He speaks to us in all things. We must make it intentional to listen for His small still voice. It will keep us from harm, it will keep us safe from those who judge unjustly, and it will lead us into fellowship with Him. For He knows the thoughts He thinks toward us; those are thoughts of peace and not of evil, and to give us an expected end. There is hope, and He is our refuge. Know that we are covered under the blood that never loses its power.

Father God, in the name of Jesus, we come before You as humble as we know how, honoring you, blessing you and worshipping You, as we enter Your gates with thanksgiving and into Your courts with praise. Father God, we lift our hands to thee and bless Your name. There is no other help we know. For You are worthy. We glorify You for Your name alone is excellent.

We come before you, Father God, with praise on our lips. Father, we come to you, oh God, with prayer in our hearts. We come to you, God, because we may be broken or lost. Oh God, we come to you because, Lord, we know that you are the way, the truth, and the life. Lord, we just come before You because we know You said to come to Jesus and to come to Him right now; to come to Jesus while we have time (Rev. Charles Nicks).

We know not the hour, nor the day, we don't know which direction to go, we don't know what to pray for, we don't know anything unless we seek Ye first the kingdom of God and Your righteousness. We don't know Father God, unless You hold our hands, Lord. We don't know unless You speak to our hearts and we hear Your small still voice. We seek You, and lean on You, and depend on You for we know that You are the author and finisher of our faith and we can't do anything without you, Lord.

We come to You because You brought us out of darkness, Father, and into Your marvelous light. We come to You Father God, because You are our teacher and our guide, so we seek You, and we cast our cares upon You. Your Word says You would never leave us nor forsake us.

We come to You, Lord, because above You, there's no other. We commit our minds to You, we submit our thoughts to You, we give You our plans, and turn our lives over to You because You are our Shepherd, and yea though we may walk through the valley of the shadow of death, we will fear no evil because You are with us. Therefore, we put our complete trust in You, Lord. Thank you, for you alone are the true and living God and everything belongs to You. In Jesus' name, Amen!

God's Light

Dear God in Jesus' name, Thank you oh God for the light, the beginning, the freshness, and the gift of a new day. We realize that if it had not been for You, we would not be able to live, move, and have our being. It is the very essence of You that we can awaken, in fact, it was You who laid us down to sleep. You kept us, You held us, You gave us peace. Without peace, we can't do anything in the fullness of Your grace.

Without peace, we cannot comprehend all that You have for us; how You made the Universe and all that exists within. How Your thoughts are higher than our thoughts. How You lined up the stars, moon, sun, and planets that they may have its own purpose; to light the darkness with stars that shines so brightly, how the moon illuminates the sky in the same place for everyone to see, how the sun warms the earth, brightens and rises for a dawning of a new day; how the planets are orbited and stands where You command.

Lord, we know that You orchestrated our lives in order the same way. You have predestined us and called us out of darkness into Your marvelous light. You've made us to be stars, the light of the world when we walk with you in obedience. As the songstress, Odetta, so sweetly sang, "this little light of mine, I'm gonna let it shine. Everywhere I go, I'm gonna let it shine. (Harry Dixon Loes)" We know that when we tap into You, You give us the light others may see. Therefore, oh God, we lift You up knowing that You will do the drawing of all men unto You. As we draw close to You, You will draw close to us. Jesus will make your crooked places straight. He can turn your life around and put your feet on solid ground; put running back in your feet, clapping in your hands and joy in your hearts. He can put a song in your spirit and turn your tears into laughter.

Stand still and see the salvation of the Lord. You may be going through a test, but He'll give you a testimony, we may not understand the trial and tribulations but remember His Words says in Proverbs to lean not to our understanding, to trust Him in all our ways and He will make our paths straight. We must give all our worries and concerns to God, who is the author and finisher of our faith. He knows all about our troubles, and if we go to Him, He will make our sorrows bright; He'll make a way out of no way. He'll turn our midnight into day, because weeping may endure for a night, but joy comes in the morning.

Continue to trust in the Lord, and He will set you free. Whom the Lord has set free, is free indeed. God can do all things but fail because He is the great I am. He is our all in all. He can move mountains just for you because you are the apple of His eyes. He thinks the world of you.

Begin to thank God in advance for the plans He has for your life knowing He will prosper you and give you hope and a future. Heavenly Father, we honor, praise, and worship You for paying the price for us while we were yet still sinners. In Jesus' name, Amen.

Talk with Jesus

It's okay to have a little talk with Jesus as the songstress says, I once was lost in sin, but Jesus took me in. And then a little light from heaven filled my soul. He bathed my heart in love and wrote my name above. You will find that a little talk with Jesus makes things right (Cleavant Derricks).

Father God in the name of Jesus, we come before you to give you thanks on this day that You have made. While rejoicing, we give thanks to You for your grace and for your mercy. Thank you for waking us up in our right minds today. Thanking you for life, for health, and for strength. Thank you, Lord, that we have movement in our bodies and our minds are healthy and clear.

Thank you, God, for a place to lay our heads and that our lying down last night was not in vain or that we didn't awaken at the judgment-seat this morning. Thank You, Lord, that we were able to get up and move about and have food on our tables to eat. Thank you for providing all our needs, God.

Thank You, Lord, for taking us to and fro, for blessing us with jobs but Lord, we know that You alone are our provider and our jobs are just our seed. Then, Lord, You kept us all day long from dangers scene and dangers unseen, from chaos, exposed mistakes, You even kept us from the arrow that flies by day and the destruction that wastes at noonday. Then you brought us back home, and we found that it was in its proper place. There was no breaking in or no going out. And even though Lord, there are storms on the ocean and that moves our way, we know that our souls are anchored in Jesus and we will not drift away (Bishop Ronald E. Brown).

Lord, we know that You calm the seas and You quiet the storms in our lives just by Your spoken Word that says, peace be still. Even the winds and the waves obey You. We thank you, oh God because You're so good to us. And we thank you, Lord, for all those who have gone before us; our parents and ancestors who introduced us to You and struggled for righteousness and stood on the foundation of Your Word that was laid for us. Lord, we are nothing without You.

Help us to think on those things that are true, noble, right, pure, lovely, and admirable in all things, as we honor you. In Jesus' name, Amen.

Our Rock

Dear Father God in Jesus' Name! Thank you once again for the opportunity to come before You and for life, health and strength. Lord, we know we can't do anything without You. Without You, we would fail. When we feel inadequate, when we feel we're not enough, when we feel our voices don't matter, remind us that we are more than conquerors through Christ Jesus who loves us, that we can do all things through Christ who strengthens us, that no weapon that is formed against us shall prosper.

Lead us to the Rock of our salvation. The Rock that will keep us from falling, the Rock that will never fail, the Rock that will never leave us nor forsake us, for when we are weak, You are strong. That Rock is Jesus, the Alpha and Omega of our being; the beginning and the end; our wheel in the middle of the wheel. Because of You, we can face tomorrow.

We can't do anything without You, oh God. Therefore, we put our trust in You, who is the author and finisher of our faith. Without You, we are nothing; without You, our lives have no meaning. Step out in faith, trusting God who knows all about You. He knows your comings and your goings; your beginnings and your endings. He knows your thoughts before you think them. He's a heart regulator, a mind fixer. He can pick you up and turn you around. He will place your feet on solid ground. We are never in too deep where He can't reach us. He will reach way down to pick you up. God specializes in healing and restoration. If you go to Him, he will pick you up; if you go to Him, He will set you free, if you go to Him, He will make you see (Tri State Mass Choir).

There's nothing too hard for Him. He is the great I am. He can do all things but fail. Try Him and see. He will put clapping in your hands, stumping in your feet, and He will show you where your purpose lies. He will stir up the gift inside of you. God is able to make all grace abound to you.

Lean not to your own understanding. Trust God in all your ways, and He will direct your paths. He wants the best for you, and He wants you to win, regardless of your situation or what you've done. He wants to heal you and set you free from bondage. The enemy wants you to stay in the box; the box of denial, the box of fear, the box of defeat, the box of sickness. But God has come to set you free from the lies of the enemy. Humble yourself, pray, seek His face, and turn from your wicked ways, and He will heal you from the inside out.

You'll look at your hands, and they will be new. You'll look at your feet, and they will be new, too. Your walk will change. Your talk will change, your company will change, and your thoughts will change. Resist the devil, and he will flee. Trust the process because God will never leave you alone and if He calls you to it, do it because He has already equipped you for the journey. Your life was predestined before you were in your mother's womb, so don't dismiss those thoughts of greatness. It's not the darkness that frightens you; it's your light. God has created you to do great things, and as you step out in faith, you liberate others to do the same (Marianne Williamson).

Go where God sends you, do what God has called you to do because you can do all things through Christ who strengthens you. God, we thank you that all things work together for the good of those who love you and who are called according to Your purpose. In Jesus' name! Amen.

Refuge

Have not I commanded thee? Be strong and of a good courage; be not afraid, neither be thou dismayed: for the Lord, thy God is with thee whitersoever thou goest.
Joshua 1:9

Our strength comes from God. Our success comes from God, as well. We can't earn it, and we can't work for it. It's all controlled by God. We must obey God even when we can't see what the results will be and when we are not certain what to do or how to do it. Set aside time each day to read and meditate on God's Word, and then remind yourself of God's Words day and night. Act today on what you know God has said, and God will strengthen you and assure your success in carrying out his purpose for your life.

Father God, in the name of Jesus, as we seek You today, we thank You for Your Word found in Psalm 46 that says that You are our refuge and strength, a very present help in trouble. Therefore, we will not fear. We will be still and know that You are God. We will not, Oh God, walk in fear over our finance, our family, our future, our health, or our faith. We will, Oh God, be still and know that what You have promised will indeed come to pass for us. We thank You, oh God, for the covering of Psalm 46, that helps us to not walk by sight when we see roadblocks, dead ends, closed doors or negative outcomes, but to walk by a faith that says, if

God be for us, who can be against us. Lord, we thank you for giving us ears to hear what you have to say. We seek the divine testimonies of Your Word, and Your divine order that we may be in good health and have complete healing. Know that you are due for physical healing in your body, spiritual healing in your soul, and an emotional breakthrough in your mind. Jeremiah 30 says that God will restore health unto thee, and He will heal thee of thy wounds.

We know that all things are possible to all that believes, and we are healed by all 39 stripes that Jesus bore on the cross at Calvary. And it's at the name of Jesus, that every knee shall bow, and every tongue shall confess that He is Lord.

Today, Lord, as we face trials and tribulations, Psalm 46 says that God is our refuge. He is our strength, a very present help in trouble. Therefore, we will not fear, though the earth be removed, and though the mountains be carried into the midst of the sea; Though the waters thereof roar and be troubled, though the mountains shake with the swelling thereof. In verse 10, He says, to be still, and know that I am God: He will be exalted among the heathen; He will be exalted in the earth. So, Lord, we ask for strength to wait on You, Lord, and to be of good courage that You will strengthen our hearts. This is my humble prayer, oh God. In Jesus' Christ's name, know that it can and will be done. Amen!

All Have Fallen Short

Even the righteousness of God which is by faith of Jesus Christ unto all and upon all them that believe: for there is no difference: for all have sinned and come short of the glory of God; being justified freely by His grace through the redemption that is in Christ Jesus.
Romans 3:22-24

Father God, in the mighty name of our Lord and Savior Jesus Christ, we humbly submit ourselves to You knowing that you are the author and finisher of our faith; knowing that we can't do anything without You; knowing that it's only because of Your grace and mercy that we are saved.

We come to You because You are the God of our salvation, above You, there is no other, and You are God and God alone. We know that you created us, You created the heavens and the earth and everything that dwells in it belongs to You.

Lord, You cause the sun to rise and the sun to set. You can do what You want, when You want, how You want and to whom You want. You bless those whom You wish and harden the hearts of those whom You choose. Lord, I thank You for choosing me. You predestined our lives and have already made a way out of no way. You already made the crooked places straight. You have already made a way of escape, and

You have blocked the enemy in his tracks, even when the enemy is within us. God, when you show Yourself to us, and we are still disobedient and unappreciative, You still provide, You still give us new mercies every day, and You still forgive us for our shortcomings. We all sin and fall short of the glory of God. Lord, because of Your grace and the price You paid on the Cross, we are made right with God and declared righteous. See, God is no respecter of persons. He is the God of everyone, and the door is opened to salvation to all.

Purge us, Lord, that we may be clean. Wash us so we may be whiter than snow. Make us hear joy and gladness; that our bones which have been broken may rejoice. I thank you, Lord, that you thought we were worth saving. So, You came and changed our lives. You thought we were worth keeping. So, You cleaned us up inside. You thought we were to die for. So, You sacrificed Your life so we could be free, and whole and tell everyone we know (Anthony Brown & group therAPy).

Lord, we praise You, we worship You, we glorify You, because You deserve it. It is You who hold our today and tomorrow in the palm of Your hands. The Lord *will give grace and glory: no good thing will he withhold from them that walk uprightly.*

So, Lord, we thank You for everything. My brother, my sister, what sin are you playing with? What thoughts are you contemplating? Are you attempting to ignore the voice of the Lord? Repent and turn from sin. Offer your life to God. Today is your day to repent! For all the wrong you have done; for the times you strayed away. Repent! For judging others; for the times we doubted the Lord. Just repent!

Our lives were created with a purpose, never allow sin to destroy it. Establish your faith in the Lord. I am convinced that nothing can separate us from the love of God. In Jesus' name, Amen.

Provider

Father God, I thank you for life, health, and strength. Thank you for making ways out of no way. Thank you for delivering us from Egypt even when we didn't want to let go. Thank you for the manna you provide and freshwater that fills us every day. It may not be the meat and potatoes we desire, but I learned a long time ago that a stomach full is a stomach full.

Your Word says, You will never leave us nor forsake us (Hebrews 13:5). If you feed the birds and they don't worry about food, You will supply our every need because You are Jehovah Jireh, our provider. You are more than enough for me (Brooklyn Tabernacle Choir).

Your truth is our shield and buckler. Knowing that gives us the confidence to go on and see what the end will be. If we give up, the enemy wins, but we are more than conquerors in Christ Jesus; our comings and goings are blessed, and no weapon that is formed against us shall prosper.

So, God, we put our trust in You because our hope is built on nothing less than Jesus' blood and righteousness, we dare not trust the sweetest frame but wholly lean on Jesus' name (Edward Mote). We thank You, God, in all things and for all the many ways you have made for us. In Jesus' name, Amen.

Stand

Dear Heavenly Father, in the perfect name of Jesus. We come before You today to give You praise, for not only showing us the way we should go but for being the way, the truth, and the life. God, thank you for the assurance of Your safety, privilege, power, and Your mercy. We realize that the dwelling place of God lies within us.

We thank you for your mercy and for your grace that covers us every day. We thank you that Your fountain is ever flowing to cleanse us from our sins. Lord, if we listen to Your still small voice, You will lead and guide us into all truth.

We know that You will open doors that were once closed in our faces. Places that denied you will begin to approve you. God will bless your thoughts. Follow God and stand on what He has said. *When you call on God, believe that He is a rewarder of them that diligently seek Him.* So, stand and if all else fails, continue to stand still until you see the salvation of the Lord.

God's *thoughts are not our thoughts, neither are His ways our ways.* Continue to stand on what God says! If He has spoken to you, it is time to be obedient. What has God spoken into your life? What has the Lord appointed you to do? Who are you waiting on? Only wait on God. When you have done all you can, and you have waited long enough, step out in faith. Take with you *the whole armor of God that ye may be able to withstand in the evil day, and having done all, to stand.*

It shall come to pass, *if thou shalt hearken diligently unto the voice of the Lord thy God, to observe and to do all His commandments, the Lord thy God will set thee on high above all nations of the earth.*

We thank You that You came to proclaim liberty to the captives and recovery of sight to the blind, to set at liberty those who are oppressed because we are destined to sit on the throne. Lord, we know that we are more than conquerors in You and if we cry out, You'll set us free. As the songstress Mahalia Jackson sung, "When I was a wretch undone, living in a world of sin. I had no hope, no peace within. Then somebody told me what Jesus did. Said He gave His life, died for my sin. Now I am justified. I am sanctified. I'll glorify His Holy name. If you come to Him, He will do the same for you. He will set you free, make you clean, give you hope, give you joy, pick you up, turn you around, place your feet on solid ground. Just come to Jesus, right now (Edwin Hawkins). Just come to Him!" In Jesus' name, we pray. Amen!

Purpose

Dear God in Jesus' name. Thank you for another opportunity to call on Your name as our Savior, our Way-maker, our Wheel in the Middle of a Wheel and our Bright and Morning Star. Although we may take it for granted and it seems to be a cliché, Your names are the very essence of our being.

God you have given us a purpose to create, recreate, succeed, overcome and tell how we got over. You have given us purpose in our mental state, emotional state, physical state, and spiritually. Your Word says when we are weak, you are strong, and we know that Nehemiah 8:10 says that the joy of the Lord is our strength.

As we walk by faith and not by sight, as we seek Ye first the Kingdom of God and His Righteousness, as we call upon You for our answers, as we lift you up, as we lean on Your understanding, we will begin to hear Your direction and discernment. You will give us peace that surpasses all understanding that will guard our hearts and minds in Christ Jesus; we will carry spiritual confidence and know who we are and who's we are, and the purpose You have for us.

God, we ask that you cover us, keep us, strengthens us, and bless us to walk away from those things, situations, and people that hinder our growth and fulfilling our purpose in You. Thank you, God, that You have not given us the spirit of fear but of love, power, and a sound mind. Because of You, we can do all things through Christ who strengthens us, and our comings and goings are blessed.

Thank you that our pain has purpose and we have to trust the process. Lord, it may not feel good, and others may talk about us, walk away from us and treat us differently, but we thank you for sanctifying us for Your purpose.

Thank You for making our enemies our footstool, seating us at the table before our enemies, and anointing our heads with oil in the presence of your enemies. Jeremiah 29:11 says that God knows the plans He has for our lives; to prosper us and to be in good health. We know that You are omnipresent, omnipotent, omniscient, and You are more than enough.

We thank You for carrying us in our times of sorrow and loneliness, I thank you for forgiving us in our disobedience. We thank You for keeping us when we were too lost to keep ourselves, God, we thank you for protecting us from the enemy and when we go astray; we thank You for Your saving grace. We give You the honor, the glory, and all the praise. For we can't do anything without You. In Jesus' name, we pray. Amen.

Thanks

Father God in Jesus' name, we thank You for the opportunity to be in Your presence, to bow before You in prayer, to thank You for another day. Lord, You called our names, and our eyes opened. What a blessed miracle to be here among the living; another chance and another opportunity to be ambassadors for You. I pray that You order our steps, I pray that our hearts and minds hear and receive Your direction for today; that we are leaning and depending on You to walk in our purpose.

Only You, Lord can make our crooked places straight; only You Lord can open new doors and pour out blessings that we don't have room enough to receive. And God when You close doors, let us not grow weary in well-doing; remind us through Your Word that weeping may endure for a night, but joy comes in the morning. Remind us that Nehemiah 8:10 says the joy of the Lord is our strength.

We know that a closed door is not always a "no", a closed door may be to wait on You, be of good courage that You may strengthen your hearts and minds. We know that it's already done. Victory is already done. Peace is already made. Deliverance is already done. The new job is on the way. That new house is on the way. That disobedient child is on the way. That bad marriage is healed, sickness and diseases are healed. Depression is healed. Anger is set free. Loneliness is set free, and no weapon formed against us will prosper.

We thank you God that You have already predestined our lives to walk in Your favor; To be above and not beneath; To walk on the serpent's head and to be more than conquerors through Christ Jesus. We thank You for life, health and strength. We thank You for Your amazing grace and undeserving mercy. Without Your grace, we would have been consumed by now. Without Your grace, we would have gotten what we really deserved.

Thank you, God, for another chance and for new beginnings. You've been better to us than we've been to ourselves. You saw fit to call our names, so we thank You for choosing us from the belly of our mother's womb. You already knew our names and our destiny. Sometimes we forget our names, but like the prodigal son, You allow us to soar our royal oats until we come back to ourselves and remember that You have everything we need. And oh God, You welcome us back into Your royal family where the feast of the Lord is going on.

Thank You, God, for never leaving us alone or forsaking us. Thank You for looking beyond our faults and seeing our needs. Thank You for looking at our hearts, as men look on the outside. Help us to lean not to our own understanding but to trust You in all thy ways that You may direct our paths. God, we know that you reign on the just as well as the unjust. You have no respecter of persons. Help us to be Your hands and feet to be a blessing to others. Comfort hurting hearts and spirits. Strengthen us, as You are the lifter of our heads. Thank you for being our solid rock that never fails.

Thank You for Your grace and mercy. Lord, we thank You in all things and through all things. We can't do anything without You. Thank You, God, in Jesus' name, Amen.

Strength

Do not sweep my soul away with sinners
Psalms 26:9

Lord, we know that you did not give us the spirit of fear. Just as David feared for his life and prayed from anxiety because of his past sin, we also wonder if all our sins will be pardoned or remembered. Because of our weaknesses, lack of faith, little courage, little love, and the many temptations, it brings on a fear that we may not enter the realm of the saved. We may find ourselves praying to God, please don't sweep our souls away with sinners or unbelievers. But be not dismayed, whatever betide, know that God will take care of you and He will not sweep His children away with sinners. Continue to walk with outward integrity and inwardly trusting in the Lord?

Dear God, our Father, we thank you for ripping the veil that we can approach the altar with humble hope and hearts as *we seek ye first the Kingdom of God and Your righteousness, that all things may be added unto us.* Lord, please give us patience to not give up and the strength to stand strong in Your Word as those who have gone before us.

Lord, you have told us not to fear. But Lord, although we trust You, we also fear that we may die without hitting the mark of the high calling, while settling for mediocrity, or fear of settling for less than Your best for our lives. Help us to resist the devil that he may flee and that he may not talk us out of what You have in store for us. We know the devil comes to kill, steal, and to destroy or bring trouble, confusion, and chaos. But, God, You can deliver us out of the hands of the enemy every time. The bible says to resist the devil, and he will flee. Teach us to trust You, God, for the strength to endure difficulties and the faith to wait for You.

Help us not to be conformed to this world but transformed by the renewing of our minds; knowing that God is able to make all grace abound toward us, having all sufficiency in all things. It's only by God's grace that the joy of the Lord is our strength. Although things may change, and we feel all alone, and our hearts are broken, the *Lord's hand is not shortened, that it cannot save; neither His ear heavy that it cannot hear*.

Lord, help us to defeat the lies of the devil with Your truth. Help us to live boldly and believe that we are *fearfully and wonderfully made* and to be *confident that He who has begun a good work in us will complete it until the day of Jesus Christ*. These blessings we entrust in Jesus' name, Amen.

God be Glory

If any man speak, let him speak as the oracles of God; if any man minister, let him do it as of the ability which God gives: that God in all things may be glorified through Jesus Christ, to whom be praise and dominion forever and ever.
1 Peter 4:11

How is God glorified when we use our abilities? He is glorified when we use them as He directs us to help others. Only then, they will see Jesus and praise Him for help they have received. Peter said to let your light so shine before men, that they may see your good works and glorify your Father which is in heaven. God is able.

Father God, in the name of Jesus. Oh Lord, we come to You boldly, we come to You hastily, we come to You confidently, and we come with expectancy because we know without a doubt that You are Lord and that You are God. We heard Your voice that said come unto me, come all who labor and are weary, and I will give you rest. For My yoke is easy, and my burden is light.

We know that You are God and is able to do just what You said You would do. We know that You will fulfill every promise to us. We know that You are able to do exceeding and abundantly above all that we can ask or imagine. You are able to be Lord over your life. We know, Lord, that you have not given us the spirit of fear but of love, power and of a sound mind. We are encouraged in knowing that You will bless us, give us breakthrough, favor, opportunities, opened doors, and give us supernatural healing that will erase years of frustration that ruled in our lives.

God, Your Word says Your blessings will run us down and take us over. So, Heavenly Father, we pray to grow spiritually and be more like You. We choose to trust You in times of adversity knowing that You are working things out for our good.

Lord, please renew a right attitude within us so we can walk upright in Your Kingdom and be true ambassadors for You. For we know that there is much work and we pray that you equip us with courage, boldness, strength, and the love of Christ to call those things that are not into existence. Knowing that anything we ask in Your name shall be done according to Your will for our lives.

Lord, we also know that our timing is not Your timing, our thoughts are not Your thoughts and our ways are not Your ways. It may be late in the midnight hour that you decide to turn it around, but we know that it's gonna work in our favor (Fred Hammond)! Isaiah says to wait upon the Lord, and He will renew our strength.

We thank You, God, for turning things around and knowing that we can run and not be weary. The Lord says, touch not my anointed and do my prophet no harm. He is a rewarder of them that diligently seek Him. Then you can sing, *God has smiled on me. He has set me free. God has smiled on me. He has been good to me* (Rev. James Cleveland). *Amazing Grace, how sweet the sound that saved a wretch like me. I once was lost, but now I'm found. Was blind but now I see* (Chris Tomlin).

Brothers and sisters, know that God is able. He is able to do just what He said He would do, and He will fulfill every promise to you. So, don't give up on God cause He won't give up on you (Darwin Hobbs). He is able. He will lead you by the still waters. He will make you lie down in green pastures. He will restore your soul. He will lead you in the paths of righteousness for His name's sake. He knows your purpose, and you will go further with God if you put Him first and make your spiritual life a priority. He would never leave you nor forsake you, so we can boldly say, "The Lord is our Helper, we will not fear what man can do unto us. In Jesus' name, we pray, Amen

At the Altar

Dear Heavenly Father, we come in Your name at this very hour, this very moment to give Your name the praise, the honor, and the glory. Knowing that this is where You hear and answer all our prayers. It's at the altar where we press our way. It's at the altar where we reach for the hem of Your garment. It's at the altar that we lay our burdens down. It's at the altar that You hear our faintest cry.

Lord, we thank You for the altar experience that we can walk away, look back and see where You have brought us from, and how You have turned things around. It's where we received our sight, and now we are happy all the day (Heritage Singers).

Lord, Your grace and Your mercy watches over us all night and all day, and we thank you God for Your Son Jesus, who died on the cross for the sins of the whole world. That's because You have all power in Your hands, it's because Your name is above every name and You can do all things except fail. Knowing this we have the very confidence in You that we can do all things in You and through You. Because of You, Lord, we give You glory, because of You, we give You praise, because of You, we can face tomorrow.

Thank you for this opportunity of prayer because we know that You hear, and you answer prayer. We know that prayer is the key that opens the door. We know that prayer changes things. We know that prayer confirms our trust and our belief in You. Thank You, that through prayer, we have the blessed assurance that Jesus is mine, oh what a forte of glory divine. Heir of salvation purchase of God, that we are born of His spirit and washed in His blood. Oh Lord, this is my story, this is my song praising my Savior all the day long (Fanny Jane Crosby).

Lord, please hear us when we call on You when we pray at Your altar. We know that Your ways are not our ways, and Your timing is not our timing. Just like You told Babylon, when seventy years were up and not a day before, that You will show up and take care of them. Your Word is true, and we stand on Your Word today.

Friends, God knows what He is doing. He has it all planned out—plans to take care of you, not abandon you, plans to give you a future and a hope (Jeremiah 29:11). Leave your prayers at the altar, and God will take care of you. In Jesus' name, Amen.

Ms. Shanell R. Burwell

Jeremiah 17:7-8
But blessed is the one who trusts in the Lord, whose confidence is in him. They will be like a tree planted by the water that sends out its roots by the stream. It does not fear when heat comes; its leaves are always green. It has no worries in a year of drought and never fails to bear fruit.

Ms. Shanell R. Burwell is a native of Durham, North Carolina. She has a BS in Psychology and minor in Biology, MS in Medical Science and MBA in Health and Administration. She has been involved in several ministries such as President of the Junior Ushers, Secretary of the Sunday School Department and

President of Single's Ministry. Currently, she is a coach and mentor of youth STEM and Robotics Ministry. She is a daughter, sister and aunt of a nephew and niece that she loves to spoil at times.

Inspiration

My biggest source of inspiration for this project, Greater Works, came from challenges I have faced in life, along with a strong inner desire to help others. I have had obstacles in my personal and professional life which I could not have conquered without God. Facing and overcoming these challenges have made me stronger, wiser, and brought me closer to God. So, for me, my inspiration came from every day and everywhere and I wanted to share prayers that I felt would help others connect with God.

For example, I recall how God got my attention in the year 2013 of December while scrolling through my social media page. Among all of the works and posts, my attention was drawn to "The Prayer Project," a challenge that started in January 2014 that was created by @Saunyaaa www.aloveperfect.com. The instructions were to select an individual and anonymously commit to composing one prayer-a-day for thirty days. I was inspired to go beyond the call and therefore, chose three people to send God's message of hope, encouragement, and healing on behalf of God.

At the end of the challenge, I presented the prayer journal as a gift to each individual to be blessed with their own personal message from God. During this intercession, I could visibly see and feel God's presence through people, nature and objects. I felt connected with the spirit and longed to get back to that space and environment.

God further prepared me for this journey by allowing a special conversation to occur with a friend which further motivated and inspired me to help others. So, when the call came to participate as an author in this project, it got my heart pumping and creative spirit working. It was an inspiration and confirmation that God had opened the door for me to continue in my mission to share and bless others.

While I was initially hesitant to take this project on, I knew the Holy Spirit would strengthen me, and I would find inspiration from my everyday life experiences that would help others. Ultimately, this experience has taught me how humility, understanding and a selfless act of love for another can be a personal benefit, as well.

Scripture: **Romans 8:26-27**
In the same way, the spirit helps us in our weakness. We do not know what we ought to pray for, but the spirit himself intercedes for us with groans that words cannot express. And he who search our hearts knows the mind of the spirit because the spirit intercedes for the saints in accordance with God's will.

Prayer Is Powerful

Prayer breaks the yoke on the enemy
Prayer changes things
Prayer makes demons tremble
Be relentless in your praying
Pray frantically as if your life depended on it
Then sit back and watch God move and
Be prepared to receive more than you could ever ask for.

Relationship

Oh, Heavenly Father, how I yearn for more of You!
Fill me up with Your presence.
Come into my body, mind and soul.
Order my steps.
Fill my mind and spirit with the Tree of Life.
I thirst for better discernment of good and evil.
I seek to get closer to You and commune with You.
Oh Lord, hear my cry.
Make my thoughts Your thoughts and let it be pleasing in Your sight.

Cover me, oh God.
Build me up with a new desire to do Your Will.
I seek to be a soldier for Christ, for I am Yours.
I relinquish everything to You, for it was never mine.
I will follow You and require Your guidance in all matters and details of my life.
I need You and I am here with opened arms.
Have Your way oh Lord, for on judgment day, I yearn to hear well done, good and faithful servant Well done!
In Jesus' name. Amen.

Scripture: Revelation 22:17

Healing, The Promise of Restoration

Dear Heavenly Father, if it's Your will, restore their spirit and make their body whole again. Give them strength to let go and let God.

Way maker, touch their body and release the bondage of sickness in the midnight hour so that they may start afresh. All power, honor and glory are in Your precious name.

You are the Alpha and the Omega; the Truth and the Light. Breathe into them, oh Lord and let thy will be done. In Jesus' name. Amen.

Scripture: Jeremiah 33:6

Release the Burden

Father God, Give me strength to bear my yoke during my time of need. Help the family to be on one accord. Intercede for our loved ones. Cast out the pain, hurt and suffering if it is your will, oh Lord.

For I know Your grace and mercy is sufficient to bring us through. I ask for peace of mind, body and spirit during these turbulent times. I put my trust in You, oh God, for You are the everlasting rock. In Jesus' name, Amen.

Scripture Psalm 68:19

My Exodus

Thank You, God for giving me my release.
An opened door to a new beginning.
No more hurt, no more pain.
No more shame, no more tears, for I am free now.
I am finally able to let go and let God.
My voice is here and here to stay.
My smile and joy are back on the inside and unveiled for all to see the true me!
Thank You, God for waiting patiently on me!
I'm more confident now, standing firm in the dirt so unshakeable, undeniable, and equipped for life by my past experiences.
Blessings through my breakthrough now run over for my sister to receive.
Thank You, Lord for the brand new me! In Jesus' name. Amen.

Scripture: Exodus 14:14

My Love Letter

Father God, You are my source, my lifeline.
There is nothing that can make me feel the way You do.
You give me all I need and more.
Your love is unconditional, never wavering.
You are the only one who can right my wrongs and straighten my path.

You provide the light during my darkest moments.
You never forsake me.
When focused and in tune, I always feel Your presence.
Thankful for Your grace and mercy.
Longing for the day to be with You in eternity.

Scripture: Deuteronomy 6:5

The One Chosen By God

Dear God, I pray that You are preparing me for the one You will send me that I will spend eternity with here on earth.

Lord knows I do not want to miss out.
Help me Lord to be slow to anger when there is so much turbulence and confusion.

Open my heart to receive and let go of the trials and tribulations that others have committed to me and for those I have committed on others.

I pray that He can see and acknowledge the God in me.
If it's Your will God, I pray that I can help strengthen his weakness so that it will take us to a higher level in doing Kingdom work.

I pray that I can have a listening ear to hear his desires and needs while we walk in the purpose You have for us, oh Lord.

I pray that my touch and tone is soothing on a bad day.
I pray that our love for each other strengthens us and that our holy bond protects us from life's daggers, fears and rejections of the unknown.

I pray that I am ready to receive this great man of God. I believe You will prepare him for my needs and wants to ensure that we are fruitful in Your will. In Jesus' name. Amen.

Scripture: Hebrews 10:37 .

Collection of Souls

Oh, Heavenly Father,

I pray for the lost souls and backsliders.
Demolish all arguments and every pretension that sets itself against the knowledge of God.

Break all strongholds and show them the way, oh God.
Bring light in the darkness.
I pray that the beacon of light is aesthetically pleasing to push out all hopelessness and despair.

Make a path out of their wilderness and order their steps according to Your will and purpose. In Jesus' name. Amen.

Scripture: 2 Corinthians 10:5

Thank You

Oh, Heavenly Father, I just want to say Thank You!

> *Trust in the Lord with all your heart*
> *and lean not on your own understanding.*
> *In all your ways acknowledge Him,*
> *and he will make your path straight.*
> **Proverbs 3:5-6**

I thank You for saving me from the confusion and delivering me from the hurt and pain.

Thank You, God for Your instructions in **Romans 12:19**. My spirit was stronger than my flesh and for that I am thankful. For this was Your will!

I am thankful for the situations that brought warfare, where I felt under attack and bound by shackles.

Worldly cycles have drawn me closer to You.
For I know my blessing is waiting at the door for my future is in Your hands, oh God.

God, You worked it out according to Your will and Your way for You didn't have to but You did.
So, I say thank You.

I have seen the protection You have provided over my life and how You have handled me so delicately.
So, I say thank You.

I know You are the source of my strength and the reason I have conquered life's challenges.
So, I say thank You.

I release and fall on my knees giving all praise and glory to You. I am so blessed; You have given me so much favor and I am truly indebted to You, oh God! And for that I say thank You. In Jesus' name, Amen!

Righteousness Through Faith

Glory be to God! Thank You for waking us up this morning clothed in our right minds and giving us another opportunity to do Your will. For we are not to allow the world to set our Godly standards. For I know better days are coming, oh God.

Faith is believing in You when it's unknown, unseen and so daunting.

Faith is surrendering our burdens to You Oh God, for You are the one who has written our story and established Your divine outcome.

As we know, troubles don't last always and joy comes at the breaking of a new day.

We sing praises and lift our hands like wings to the heavens to glorify Your name.

God, we thank You for setting the table for us to partake in the bread of life.

I urge my brothers and sisters to seek provisions through scripture, for God gives us truth.

I ask that You help us do better and be better today than we were yesterday.

I pray for the body of Christ to be a blessing for someone today that sparks the light and unveils the spirit.
In Jesus' name, Amen!

Scripture: Romans 12:2 John 6:35

The Key to Discernment

Dear God. Give us discernment over good and evil. We desire clarity and peace over our circumstances. Release the struggle of affliction. For we all have sinned and are all flawed but let us be recognized by the fruit, we bare through love, kindness and faithfulness, oh Lord.

We require discernment over every area of our life to govern in Your authority. For we seek wisdom and restoration in the face of opposition. For faith comes by hearing and not by sight for we discerned carefully on who speaks into our ear. We no longer want to miss out.

For every step is a blessing and we will press on through praise. We will apply every principle, for faith without works is dead. For everything that was lost was not needed to bless us. For grace abounds in the living waters. In Jesus' name, Amen.

Scriptures: Matthew 7:16-20, Galatians 5:22-23 and Psalm 169-176

Deaconess Karen A. Middleton

Ephesians 2:10 (NIV)
For we are God's handiwork, created in Christ Jesus to do good works, which God prepared in advance for us to do.

Deaconess Karen A. Middleton is a native of Charleston SC and is married to the esteemed Deacon Henry C. Middleton. From this union, they have five beautiful children and six adorable grandchildren. She is the 5th child of 11 children. She has been a member of Mt. Moriah Missionary Baptist Church for 21 years. Karen faithfully serves as an Advisor of the Young Children's Choir for 20 years. She certainly has a special place in her heart for the young people. Most of her volunteer work reaches in the community where she serves as a mentor to many and serving in community health fairs. Whenever you see her, you can count on being inspired by her smile, wittiness a word of encouragement and inspiration.

Karen has been employed for 19 years as a Clinical Supervisor at Charleston Women's Wellness Center under the direction of Dr. Paula E. Orr, MD. Karen obtained her NRCMA certification in 2015. On December 16, 2017, she obtained her Bachelor of Science Degree in Human Services from Springfield College, Massachusetts (Charleston Site). She attained the Dean's list and graduated Magna Cum Laude. Karen is currently enrolled in theology classes through Morris College of South Carolina, where she is studying and rightly dividing the Word of God. Although Karen has never written a book, she gives special thanks to the Holy Spirit for choosing her as a co-author of His inspiring book.

Inspiration

I was inspired by the Holy Spirit through a dear friend of mine to write down my prayers. It never occurred to me to write my prayers for others to read. However, I was reminded that Paul wrote a letter to the church of Philippi, reminding the people to stand firm during persecution and rejoice regardless of circumstances.

In the same letter, Paul warns them about satanic forces that linger among them. If God used Paul, He sure could use me to encourage and give hope to the hopeless. I thank God for allowing me such a time as this to encourage others who may be struggling or walking haphazardly through their journey of life. God allowed me to write my prayers because I've either experienced or am experiencing seasons in my life and can encourage someone to stand firm and see the Glory of God while you are in your season.

I pray that before you read these prayers, humble yourselves before the Lord, repent and give Him all of you. Then, allow God to lead you to a prayer that speaks to your situation.

Wherever you are in your faith and seasons of life, remember these words a songwriter wrote; "The tempest is raging, the billows are tossing high, the sky is shadowed with blackness and no shelter or help is nigh. Just have faith to know that God will speak "Peace Be Still" to and through your seasons."

Be encouraged…

What, after all, is Apollos? And what is Paul? Only servants, through whom you came to believe – as the Lord has assigned to each his task. I planted the seed, Apollos watered it, but God has been making it grow.
1 Corinthians 3:5-6 (NIV)

"**Blessed assurance, Jesus is mine!** O what a foretaste of glory divine! Heir of salvation, purchase of God, born of His spirit, washed in His blood" (Crosby, F. 1873).

At the Altar

Father in heaven, thank You for allowing me this time of solitude to come in Your presence. I know that while I'm here, I can find refuge for my soul: peace, rest, answers to my prayers, corrections, deliverance, healing, and restoration. Oh, it is so sweet to abide in You when all things are good and when I feel like all hell is breaking loose. Father, I humbly and boldly bow my heart to Your feet. While I'm here, I am tightly holding on to Your garment and not letting go.

Father at times, it seems hard for me to see You through all my hurt and disappointments. I recognize that my storms are demonic spirits severing as detours to block me from getting to You. You know all about me. You created me in Your own image. You know my coming and going. You know my thoughts, wants, desires, and needs.

Even though You did not give me the spirit of fear, I am afraid of who I will lose as I travel this journey. I can't see where You're taking me, but I trust You. I may not know the plans You have for me, but You know the plans You have for me. Through it all, I now know what it really feels like to pick up my bed and follow You. And, for me to deny my flesh from what and who I love, I must lose somethings and even some people along this journey.

I realized, the very things I hold dear to my heart, either they belong to You or have no place for Your glory. Father, for me to get to You, I know I must make sacrifices. I humbly lay it ALL at Your feet! I am willing to lose it only for You to get Your Glory! You have all power in Your hands. I am an altar for You!

Thank You, Holy Spirit, for giving me the boldness to make sacrifices and put it All on the altar. Those things/people I lost, God I know You will restore if it is Your will for Your Glory and my life. Father, I realized, those things were blocking my path from getting to You. Father, You created me to worship You! I know, You will get Your Glory out of this!

On this journey, You are allowing those things to grow me spiritually while purifying my heart. Even though I feel the pushing, pain, burning, and the pressure, they all are for Your Glory and my good.

Father, You are growing me more in Your Word and into whom You created me to be.

What a Sovereign and Divine King You are! Do what You do best, Lord! Thank You for the fire in my season. Lord, I know it is only temporary, and fire is allowing me to see my purpose-driven life. Father, I ask that You continue guiding and ordering my steps for Your Glory.

In the book of Philippians 1:6 (KJV), "Being confident of this very thing, that He which hath begun a good work in you will perform it until the day of Jesus Christ." Father, I trust You and give You all the Glory, Praise, and the Honor because You are Worthy of all my praise.

In Jesus' name, Amen!

One thing have I desired of the Lord, that will I seek after: that I may dwell in the house of the Lord all the days of my life, to behold the beauty of the Lord and to enquire in His temple.
Psalm 27:4 (KJV)

Free from Unrighteousness

Father, I am a wretched sinner standing on shaky ground. I found myself standing on my own promises and the promises of others. Looking away from what was/is right while looking for love and validation in people in all the wrong ways. 1st John 1:9 tells me that "if I confess my sins, You are faithful and just and You will forgive my sins and purify me from all unrighteousness."

Father, forgive me for not putting my trust totally in You. I surrender my heart to You so that You can wash me whiter than snow and free me from the bondages that are holding me captive. I no longer want to be separated from Your love. I remember a songwriter says, "On Christ, the Solid Rock I stand, all other ground is sinking sand."

Thank You for loving me even when I didn't deserve Your love. Thank You for saving me when I didn't deserve it. Thank You for loving me when I thought I was unlovable. Father, I thank You for setting me free from the very things that separated me from You. Now Lord, if You so please, order my steps for Your glory. I belong to You, Lord. Guide me to be whom You created me to be. Give me the boldness to stand for righteousness, even if I must stand alone. I know You are here with me and I surrender all my being to You, Lord. Thank You for hearing my prayer. In Jesus' name, Amen.

The LORD is my light and my salvation; whom shall, I fear? The LORD is the stronghold of my life; of whom shall I be afraid?
Psalm 27:19ESV

Divine Protection

Holy Spirit, You are welcome in this temple. I am before You and want nothing to hinder my worship with You. I strip all of me in Your presence: my mind, thoughts, desires, wants, need, hurts, disappointments, sickness, and issues. Whatever it is, You can have it all. Yet, in spite of myself and through my tribulations, You stayed right by my side. Through my dark days, You allowed me to see the light ahead so I can find my way back to the cross. I can look up and see Your beauty all around me. No matter what it looks like, You get Your glory. No matter what I see, You get Your glory. Jesus, I thank You for leaving the Holy Spirit as my comforter and divine protection over my life.
In Jesus' name, Amen.

*Keep me as the apple of the eye,
hide me under the shadow of thy wings.*
Psalm 17:8 (KJV)

Unconditional Love

Father Almighty, maker of heaven and earth, You are my rock and shield. A present help in the time of trouble. You in Your Glory, left the Holy spirit as a comforter to dwell with me. Father, I thank You and will forever praise You. You are the epitome of Greatness! No one else can take Your place. I don't deserve Your love, but because You first love me, You thought it not robbery or selfish to give Your Son as a living sacrifice for me. Oh, what a love. Thank You for Your unfailing love.
In Jesus' name, Amen.

Create in me a clean heart, O God, And renew a steadfast spirit within me.'
Psalm 51:10 (NASB)

Purify Me

Jesus, You are the potter, and I am just a clump of clay. I thank You for molding and shaping me for Your glory. No! It does not feel good. Yes! It is uncomfortable, but I know it's all for Your glory. Even when I can't see my way, I know the Holy Spirit is guiding me through it all.

Thank You for chipping away the things that do not glorify You. Father, I know when You are finished, I will be as pure gold, shining in Your light. Father, I don't want the world to see me; clothing, face, makeup, car, etc. I want them to see You who dwell and shineth in me. In Jesus' name, Amen.

> *Ye have heard that it hath been said, Thou shalt love thy neighbor, and hate thine enemy. But I say unto you, Love your enemies, bless them that curse you, do good to them that hate you, and pray for those who despitefully use you, and persecute you; That ye may be the children of your Father who is in heaven: for he maketh his sun to rise on the evil and on the good, and sendeth rain on the just and on the unjust. For if ye love them which love you, what reward have ye? Do not even the publicans the same? And if ye salute your brethren only, what do ye more than others? Do not even the publicans so?*
> **Matthew 5:43-47 (KJV)**

Blessings for My Enemies

Father, thank You for allowing me this day and time to come before Your presence with thanksgiving. Before I ask You for anything, Father search my heart. I know that You're going to find something. Father, those things that do not bring glory to Your name, please cast it out to the sea of forgetfulness where they never to return.

Father, Your Word says in James 5:16, "the effectual fervent prayer of the righteousness man availeth much." Before I utter a prayer for my brothers, sisters, family, enemies, and friends, my heart must be in the right condition.

Father wash my heart from all unrighteousness. If there is anyone I have hurt through my words, actions, innuendos, or other misdoings, please forgive me and allow me to go back and make it right for Your glory. Father, when I pray, I am confident to know that You hear my prayer.

Father, I lift my family to You. Whatsoever they stand in the need of, I know You will supply their needs. I lift my friends to You. Cover, heal, deliver, and set the captive free from whatever has them bound.

Father, I pray a blessing on my enemies today. Father, I know You said in Your Word that vengeance is Yours, but I pray that You hold back Your wrath from my enemies. I pray that You heal them from all their unrighteousness and bring to their remembrance any wretched deeds so that they can make it right with You. I stand boldly before You to forgive them for they know not what they do. Break stony hearts and strengthen them for Your glory.

Father, You are love. Therefore, You love me. So, Father continue to give me the spirit of love to bless and love my enemies. Father, I give You all the praise, honor, and, glory. In Jesus' name, Amen.

The Lord is close to the brokenhearted and saves those who are crushed in spirit.
Psalm 34:18 NIV)

Widows and Widowers

Almighty God, I lift-up widows and widowers to You. Father, I pray a special covering for widows and widowers. Father, remind them that they are never alone. Allow them to live with the memories of their loved one until that great getting up morning where they too will meet them in glory.

Father, we know that we all will travel this path, but we are asking You to make their pathway straight, fill that void with love and peace that surpasses understanding. Mend broken and lonely hearts. Restore their joy and hope for tomorrow. Give them the strength and desire to stay focused on You, Lord and to see what the end is going to be. Now Lord, send someone their way to remind them that they are not alone. In Jesus' name, Amen.

Love is patient, love is kind. It does not envy, it does not boast, it is not proud. It does not dishonor others, it is not self-seeking, it is not easily angered, it keeps no record of wrongs. Love does not delight in evil but rejoices with the truth. It always protects, always trusts, always hopes, always perseveres. Love never fails. But where there are prophecies, they will cease; where there are tongues, they will be stilled; where there is knowledge, it will pass away.
1 Corinthians 13:4-8 (NIV)

Prayer for Family

Father, I come standing in the gap for my family today. I am calling on You today. No other name I know. Father, I lift my family up to You; just in case they forgot to thank You for waking them up this morning. Just in case, they didn't thank You for the food they ate today. Just in case, they forgot to acknowledge You on the highways and by-ways. Just in case, they boasted about their ability and strength. Just in case, they did not yield to temptation or to Your command. Just in case, they may have hurt someone today. Father, just in case, they did not say yes to Your way and Your will. I will stand before You and say Thank You, Jesus!

Father, please forgive them of all unrighteousness. Speak to each heart today and if You so please mend broken spirits. Deliver one-sided minds and allow them to focus on You and not things of this world. Father, You say if we keep our minds stayed on thee, You will keep us in perfect peace. I believe Your Word and trust Your promises.

Father, I speak deliverance for those being held captive from the strongholds of life: child molestation, disappointments, hurt, drugs, alcohol, self-boasting, fornication, adultery, lust, lover of money, envy, jealousy, gossip, sickness, vain thinking, depression, self-pleasing. Father, restore love in families today. I declare and decree that the captives will be loose and set free in the name of Jesus, Amen.

You will keep him in perfect peace, whose mind is stayed on you because he trusts you.
Isaiah 26:3 (NIV)

Peace

Jesus, I come boldly to Your throne of mercy and grace. My soul cries out, "Yes" to Your will and Your way! Father, I know it will cost me something, but as long as I have You, I have everything I need. As I carry my cross to follow You, Father, I will trust You with all my being. Have Your way in and through my life today. Father, I ask that You hide me behind Your cross. Whatever my assignment is today, give me the peace, strength, and the courage to stand and let it be pleasing in Your sight.

Father, give me the words that You will have me to say to bring a lost sheep back home. Father, I speak against anything and anyone that will try to hinder me from completing my assignment. Have Your way! In Jesus' name, Amen.

He shall call upon Me, and I will answer him; I will be with him in trouble; I will deliver him and honor him. With long life, I will satisfy him, And show him My salvation."
Psalm 91:15-16

A Troubled Heart

Father, I woke up this morning with praises on my lips and my bitter cup. I feel a load bearing down so heavy. But I was reminded as a songwriter says; "I feel like a ship that's tossed and driven, battered by an angry sea. When the storms of life are raging, and their fury falls on me, I wonder Lord, I wonder, what have I done to make this race so hard to run." I tried Lord, to do the best in service and to live the best I can.

Father, I try to do the right thing but evil's present on every hand. There are misunderstandings out of all the good I do. I go to my friends for consolation and find them complaining too. I wonder Lord, what today will bring." The Holy Spirit spoke to my heart and said, "don't worry, The Lord will make a way somehow."

Father, I am comforted to know that nothing catches You by surprise. Father, You said in Isaiah 54:17, "No weapon that is formed against thee shall prosper; and every tongue that shall rise against thee in judgment thou shalt condemn. This is the heritage of the servants of the LORD, and their righteousness is of me, saith the LORD."

Father, thank You for Your Word of assurance and Your divine protection for my soul. Now, lead me Lord to that secret place in You. In Jesus' name, Amen.

For we do not have a High Priest who is unable empathize with our weaknesses, but we have one who has been tempted in every way, just as we.
Hebrews 4:15 (NIV)

My Daily Assignment

Father, thank You for this day, my daily bread. A day I will never see again. Thank You for allowing me to wake up for Your glory. Father, as I embark on what You will have me to do, keep me focused and knowing that You are my protector. In my weakness, You are strong, so speak through me to Your people.

Father, allow Your words to penetrate through hardened hearts, heal broken spirits, cover confused minds, heal diseases, deliver and set someone free from demonic spirits. Father, in Your name, I rebuke any distractions that would try to hinder me from doing Your will. Father, You get Your glory through all I do and say today. In Jesus' name, Amen.

Wait on the Lord: Be of good courage, And He shall strengthen Your heart: Wait, I say, on the Lord!
Psalm 27: 14

Anxiousness

Father, when I feel anxious about anything, slow me down enough to hear Your voice. When I feel tired and weak, give me the strength I need to carry on. When I am confused and can't seem to find my way, speak to my mind, and make my pathway clear. When I am hesitant and too nervous to move forward, Father, give me the courage to put one foot in front of the other. You did not give me the spirit of fear, but of a sound mind for Your glory.

Now Lord, help me to stay focused and wait to hear from You. Keep my feet planted until You are ready for me to walk in Your way. Thank You for the way, the truth and the light. In Jesus' name, Amen.

Do not conform to the pattern of this world but be transformed by the renewing of your mind. Then you will be able to test and approve what God's will is- His good, pleasing and perfect will.
Romans 12:2 (NIV)

Encouragement

Father God, I am not always in control of the thoughts that enter my mind. I want to hear from You, but I find myself hearing too many distractions. My vision is cloudy, and my mind is foggy. Father, I ask for a fresh anointing over my life in the name of Jesus. Saturate all of me so that I can move forward in You.

Father, shield my eyes and my mouth so I can see You and hear You. Father, when I feel that I can't go on, I know with You all things are possible. When the devil tries to tell me otherwise, I know that I am more than a conqueror through You who strengthens me. In Your Word, 1 Peter 2:9 tells me that I am a chosen people, a royal priesthood, a holy nation, God's possession, that I may declare the praises of him who called me out of darkness into His wonderful light.

I declare and believe by faith that I was made to worship You, and the devil is a liar. Thank You, Lord, for a renewed mind and spirit. In Jesus' name, Amen.

I will not leave you comfortless: I will come to you.
John 14:18 (KJV)

The Loss of a Loved One

Father, I thank You that I can come to You just as I am. My heart is in turmoil, and I don't know what to say or what to pray for. Father, I loved _____, and I know You loved _____ best. My heart is torn up inside and at times feels like I can't go on. I find it hard to simply take a breath. I know Your Word said, to be absent from the body is to be present with You. I know we must travel this route. I know we should be preparing for our final departure. I know death is the beginning of our journey to heaven. Father, I can truthfully say, I am struggling with this. I am missing _____ and need You to cover me and heal my broken heart. I thank You for trusting _____ in my care for ____ years. I pray that You were pleased with my service. I realize my assignment is over and _____ is resting and waiting for the trumpet to sound. Father lean my back against Zion wall and hide me in Your loving arms. I need You. I can't make it without You holding my hands. I stand before You for strength and comfort. Thank You, Lord, for hearing my prayer. In Jesus' name, Amen

The lord is my life and my salvation, whom shall, I fear? The Lord is the stronghold of my life – of whom shall I be afraid? 2 When the wicked advance against me to devour me, it is my enemies and my foes who will stumble and fall.
Psalm 27:1-2 NIV

Strength in The Storm

Father, there is a storm out on the ocean, and it has moved my way. I am reminded that if my soul is not anchored in Jesus, I will surely drift away. Lord, God, Father in heaven, maker of heaven and earth. I don't want my soul to drift away.

Father, it seems like when I do the right things, satan barrels down on me. When I don't give in to the enemy's scheme, he tries to rise a little higher. He uses people that supposed to love me. Those that I trusted to do the right thing. Those I adore and showed mercy to.

Father in my flesh, I want to throw in the towel. I know that if I give in, I will say and do things that are not pleasing in Your sight. This pain and disappointment run deep beyond recovery. I asked that You protect, strengthen, and heal my broken heart.

Father, I know this storm did not catch You by surprise. But I am reminded through the Holy Spirit that if I keep my mind stayed on You, You will keep me in perfect peace. I am also reminded to look to the hills for where my help comes. I know my Help comes from

You, Lord! You said storms come to make me strong. Right now, I don't feel so strong, but I know You are yet molding me and removing things and people that do not represent You.

Father, I know You love me, and I trust You with my life. Thank You for Your mercy and grace for my life. In Isaiah 54:17, Your Word said, "No weapon that is formed against me shall prosper, and every tongue that shall rise against thee in judgment thou shall condemn. This is the heritage of the servants of the Lord, and their righteousness is of me, saith the Lord." Father, I trust in You, and I know Your Word will not return void.

Father, as I continue to walk in my purpose, continue to stir up the gift You've equipped in me because I want to please You and make You smile. Father, I've got my war clothes on and will continue to stay properly dress. Now Lord, give me the spirit of love like You love. Allow me to see and grow through this. This is Your servants prayer. In Jesus' name, Amen.

If my people, which are called by my name, shall humble themselves, and pray, and seek my face, and turn from their wicked ways; then will I hear from heaven, and will forgive their sin, and will heal their land.
2 Chronicles 7:14 (KJV)

Corporate Prayer

Father, I come before you to lift the world to you. Father, I know you did not give us the spirit of fear, but of a sound mind. As we look and hear what is happening around us, we can see the devil and his adversaries are trying to put fear in our hearts and mind. In some of us, he has succeeded. Father, I pray for families who lost loved ones and those who were injured for selfish gains. I pray for children and their families who are held captive for political gains.

Father, I lift the leaders that are in positions to make a change and speak peace. Father, I ask that You speak to their hearts, deliver, and set them free from their pride, evil, and selfish gains. This world is not our home, and it only belongs to You, Lord. I pray stony hearts are broken. I pray for deliverance, peace, love and those who do not know You for the free pardoning of their sins. Father, I pray for the backsliders that they surrender all to You and return to (You) their first love. Father, I will continue to stand in the gap for those brothers and sisters who lost their way. Thank You,

Lord, for allowing me to stand firmly and boldly for Your glory. My pray is if only one return to You, I will rejoice and give You all the glory, honor, and praise. In Jesus' name, I pray, Amen.

Therefore, we are buried with him by baptism into death: that like as Christ was raised up from the dead by the glory of the Father, even so, we also should walk in newness of life. For if we have been planted together in the likeness of his death, we shall also be in the likeness of his resurrection.
Romans 6: 4-5

Give Thanks

Father, thank You for Your Son, Jesus Christ. Thank You for allowing me to walk in newness with You. Father, I lift my heart up to You for continued cleansing. I want to be obedient to Your will for my life and the life of others.

Father give me the strength to continue serving Your people. I want to make You smile, Lord.

Now Lord, order my steps, lead me, cover me, and guide me as I travel through this purpose-driven life. I was created to worship You and will continue until the trumpet sounds or until I meet You in the air.

Father, thank You for all You have done for not only myself but for my family. All belongs to You, and I leave them at Your feet.

Lord, You get Your glory out every one of their lives. You have all power to deliver and set the captive free. I trust and honor You this day. You are the Great I AM! You are the Alpha and Omega! In Jesus' name, Amen.

Rev. Patricia W. Crawford

Revelation 22:2 (KJV)
"In the midst of the street of it, and on either side of the river, was there the tree of life, which bare twelve manner of fruits, and yielded her fruit every month: and the leaves of the tree were for the healing of the nations."

Rev. Patricia W. Crawford is an Associate Minister at Mt. Moriah Missionary Baptist Church. Dedicated to serving God and His people and passionate about prayer and teaching; her ministries include Grief and Recovery, serving as the spiritual teacher for the Women's Auxiliary, and coordinator for the Upper Room Prayer ministry. She also serves as Chaplain for the Women's Clergy of the Charleston County Baptist Association. She obtained a Bachelor of Science degree in Commerce from North Carolina Central University and her Master of Public Administration from the College of Charleston and the University of South Carolina. Rev. Crawford is married to Frank Crawford, Jr. and they are the parents of two daughters, Allison C. Ford (Cody) and Kristen M. Crawford and they are the grandparents of two adorable grandsons Daniel, and Ethan Ford.

Inspiration

The urgency to participate in this writing project results from a divine inspiration from God Himself. When you are confronted with a "God wink" moment and when God gives you a personal invitation to join Him in His work; there is no alternative but to realize, as Paul says in Philippians, that "it is God who is working in you, enabling you both to will and act for His good purpose." It is not a coincidence that participating with the church in the 42 day reading of the "Purpose Driven Life" that God presented this writing opportunity that compels me to complete the writing of the last three chapters of the book that He has been waiting for me to finish. My involvement with this project confronted me with a direct command from God to finish the work! In so doing, my purpose intersects with destiny so that His will for my life is fulfilled through blessing the lives of His people.

The opportunity to write a series of prayers with Sonja Pinckney Rhodes and these wonderfully chosen and ordained women of God is an answer to prayer for my own struggles to finish the work that He assigned. Not knowing how or what to do, I prayed, and He has provided people, talent, resources, and the help needed to complete the assignment.

As He has answered my prayers time and time again, I believe that as you read these scripture based prayers that you will be inspired and reassured that God is a faithful and prayer answering God. He has solidified my call to a lifestyle of prayer and the call to minister with dedicated prayer warriors who have been called by God to the Upper Room Prayer Ministry at Mt. Moriah. I'm grateful to an awesome God who has shown me favor, along with these women, to write for His honor and glory. Surely, He has rewarded me for faithfulness to the prayer ministry as a warrior and an intercessor. May these prayers bless your life, inspire and encourage you as you make prayer a lifestyle and daily commitment to pray without ceasing. To God be all the glory!

Prayer of Praise and Worship

Oh Lord, how excellent is Your name in all the earth! You are great and greatly to be praised! Our souls do magnify and lift You up. Marvelous are Your works and that our souls know very well. The earth and all therein declare Your glory, and we bring You the sacrifice of praise. Our lips shall praise the Lord, our hearts rejoice, and our souls magnify You, Lord, for You are the great and awesome God. Truly, Lord, there is none like You in all the heavens or the earth. You are the great God, and the earth declares Your glory. Lord, You are Holy and righteous in all Your ways, and we thank You for bestowing Your blessings upon us. Through You Lord and through Your being and Your doings we know that You are God and God alone. Thank You for allowing us the privilege of drawing strength and power from You. Great is Your faithfulness unto us, and we give You thanks for the daily impartation of new mercies in our lives. Our spirits rejoice in You as we bow down in humbleness of heart to worship You in spirit and in truth.

Give us the grace, Dear Lord, to render unto You our best praise and our best worship with the excellence that You deserve. We acknowledge Your excellency and Your majesty Lord and all the days of our lives we shall lift Your name in praise and adoration. For all the good things and for all the wonderful blessings that You have bestowed upon us, we shall never forget Your works. With our whole hearts, we shall glorify Your name and honor You all the days of our lives. Our hearts rejoice in You Lord from the rising of the sun to the going down of the same for Your name is to be praised. Our souls love You, Lord, for you are the glorious redeemer and our righteous judge. Thank You for being our everlasting, and eternal God for You have rescued our lives from destruction and put praise and thanksgiving in our hearts and lives forever.

In the name of Jesus, we pray and seal this prayer. Amen.

Psalm 8, Psalm 145, Psalm 139

Prayer For Salvation

Our Lord and our God, You are not slack concerning Your promises and are not willing that any should perish, but that all should come to repentance. When the enemy snaked his way into our lives, You planned the way for our salvation, redemption, and deliverance. We thank you, Father, that from the beginning of time Your plan for our way of escape from eternal damnation was through the death of Your only begotten Son, Jesus Christ. Thank You personally for my way out of sin, darkness, and death into Your marvelous way of salvation and eternal life. Thank You, God, for loving us so much that You desired none should be lost and that we should all come to You with the inquiry "what must I do to be saved?"

Lord, we give You thanks for putting a hunger and desire in us to want to know You as Lord and Savior. Open our hearts continuously to be thankful for the gift of eternal life. Help us Lord to be bold in sharing the way of salvation with others who do not know You. Empower us to share the good news of the gospel of Jesus Christ so that others will believe and be saved. Lord let there be no fear and apprehension in telling others how we confessed with our mouths and believed in our hearts that You raised Your Son Jesus from the dead. Help us to share with those who don't have a relationship with You that the only requirement is to make that confession of belief to receive You as Lord and Savior.

Hide Your Word in our hearts so that we have an answer for everyone that needs to know that the way of salvation comes from being made right with You, Father. Thank you, Lord, for justifying, sanctifying us, and making us new in You. Help us, Lord, once we have been saved and delivered from our sins to walk in the liberty wherein we have been made free. When we stumble and fall, remind us that we have an advocate through Jesus who will restore us into right relationship with You Father. Lord, let us forever be mindful that Jesus made the ultimate sacrifice through His death on the cross so that we could avoid eternal death and live unto righteousness. Lord for these and all blessings from You, we give You thanks, praise, honor, and glory in the name of Jesus. Amen

Acts 16, Romans 10, Galatians 5

Good Success

Lord God, Holy and majestic is Your name. We call upon Your name, for You, Lord God are worthy to be praised. With our whole hearts, we will praise Your name for You are a great and awesome God! We will bless You at all times and praise Your Holy and righteous name. You alone are the great God who exercises kindness, justice, and righteousness in the earth. We give You thanks for being the triune God whose tender love and mercies are new every morning. Father, we thank You for being a faithful and dependable God who never ceases to amaze us. You are gracious to make our ways prosperous and to give us good success as we allow Your Word to feed us and nourish us spiritually.

Father, we ask that You help us to continue to grow in knowledge of Your Word and Your truths so that we can handle the affairs of our lives wisely. Help us with our desire to be faithful and obedient in all things concerning our lives. Lord give us the ability and desire to spend more time in Your presence and in Your Word so that we might learn of Your plans and Your purposes. Father help us to align ourselves with your plans and purposes for they are not meant to harm us, but to allow us to prosper for a hope and a future. Lord, we ask that You continue to allow favor and blessings to rain down on us.

Lord, we thank You, and we praise You for guarding us from fear and worry as we pursue Your will for our lives. Give us the mind of Christ so that we might operate with a mind of clarity, excellency, and accuracy. Remind us that the promises of the Lord are yes and amen and that what You have spoken and ordained for our lives shall come to pass. Your favor surrounds us at all times and in all places as we represent You in the Kingdom. You have made us stable and secure in our occupations and in our ministries.

Thank You, Lord, for giving us the ability to excel in our performance and to succeed in our assignments. You give us power and might; You give us confidence and assurance, and so we trust You Lord with the fulfillment of our destinies. Lord it is You that protects our hearts, our minds, our character, our esteem, and our reputations so that we remain successful in our ability to accomplish our missions on the earth. Father, our minds rest in knowing that You are in control of all of the details of our lives and every aspect of our existence. We rely on You for continued success and we give You thanks for answered prayers. Amen

Jeremiah 29, II Corinthians 1

Direction

Father God, we come once again with praise and thanksgiving to seek You for direction. Thank You for giving us a roadmap in Your Word that admonishes us to trust in You with our whole hearts and to lean not unto our own understanding. We are blessed in knowing that if we acknowledge You in all our ways, You will most assuredly direct our paths. Your Word is a light unto our paths and a lamp unto our feet that shows us the way in darkness. You are our helper and our guide, and we need never worry when You lead us in the paths of righteousness. When our ways seem dark and dreary, You are the source of light that brings us to a place of safety. We realize Lord that except You guide us and direct our paths, we will be lost and drifting in a place of hopelessness and despair. You are the source of all that we need in life.

Thank You, Lord, for the times that we don't have answers for the problems and circumstances that confront us, but yet You come to our rescue. We ask that You continue to walk with us in times of fear, frustration, anxiety, and distress. Walk with us in times of confusion and discord. Be our guide, Lord in times of uncertainty and doubt. Let Psalm 91 and the name of our God Jehovah-Nissi be the banner of direction over our lives. Give the angelic host charge to hover over us and to accompany us on this journey of life.

Continuously keep us hidden under the shadow of Your wings, keep us close to Your bosom and keep us hidden until the calamities of life pass. Give us continued wisdom and revelation for direction in the critical times of need in our lives.

Lord, we acknowledge that it is You and You alone who orders our steps and establishes us in Your ways so that our feet do not stray. We are Your sheep, and You are our shepherd, lead us Lord in the way that we ought to go. Let Your rod and Your staff continue to guide us. Father, we ask that You continue to comfort us. Lord, let our hearts continue to delight in You so that we never wander aimlessly in life. Keep us from drifting and floating through life as desert tumbleweeds so that we never accomplish the purposes that You have ordained.

Thank You for being the God who makes our darkness light and our crooked ways straight. Let Your will be done in our lives. Remind us time and time again that You Lord are our very present help who rescues us when we lose our direction. Thank You for being our advocate and our intercessor who gives us words of comfort as You assure us that You are with us always and will never leave us nor forsake us. We trust You, Lord, to continue to show us the way and to continually lead us in the paths of righteousness. Thank You for Your blessed assurance and for Your spirit that leads us into all truth. We bless You and praise Your name forever and ever. Amen.

Proverbs 3, Psalm 119, Hebrews 13

Meet the Needs

Great, eternal, and everlasting God our Father, the one who has promised to be a very present help in the time of our needs, we enter into Your presence to give You thanks and adoration. Thank You for being a prayer answering God, who knows what we need even before we ask. Your Word instructs us to ask so that we will receive. Your Word informs us that we have not because we ask not. Lord, we are so grateful that You supply all of our needs according to Your riches in glory. Father, we are thankful that the earth is Yours and the fullness thereof. You own the cattle on a thousand hills, and every good and perfect gift comes from You. Thank You, Lord, that we can access the wealth that has been laid up for us as heirs and joint-heirs of our Father's riches. Continue to be the supplier of every good and perfect gift that we long for.

Father, we are thankful that You have given us good gifts and great blessings beyond our ability to fathom or to even comprehend. You, Lord, are the great Jehovah Jireh, the provider of all our needs. As El Shaddai, You are the all-sufficient one whose help is adequate for fulfilling our desires and wants. As Elohim, You have the ability to create all things in every manner that is needed. When we lack faith Lord, increase our ability to believe and to trust You to honor

Your Word so that it will do what You have commanded. Increase or faith to believe that You will do all that You have spoken, declared, and decreed over our lives.

When we are impatient and its looks as if You are not answering our prayers and meeting our needs, help us to be patient and wait on Your timing for the delivery of all that You have promised. We are thankful Lord that You have spoken blessings, favor, promises, and declarations over our lives.

Thank You for assuring us that Your word will not return to us void but will accomplish all that You intend and we know that Your Word will not return void. Father continue to help us to remember that You are the supplier of all of our needs and the only one that can grant promotion, favor, and increase in our lives. You bestow honor, riches, and blessings in the lives of Your children as part of the rich inheritance that is laid up for us.

Help us to be even more grateful and appreciative of blessing us with more than we can ask or think. Surely God if you take care of the birds of the air and the beasts of the field, You can provide us with abundant and overflowing blessings that our eyes have not seen, or our ears have not heard. Help us, Father, to never doubt You or Your Word. Help us not to doubt or be anxious about Your ability to supply our needs.

Thank You for Your provisions that assure us that if we abide in You that we can ask for anything in the name of Jesus and He will do it. Thank You for blessing us and answering our prayers for we have confidence in Your Word and Your ability to perform it for You are faithful to do what You have spoken. We give you thanks for all of Your gifts and blessings. Amen

Psalm 46, James 4, Philippians 4, Psalm 24, Psalm 50, James 1, Ezekiel 38

Protection

Oh Lord, Our God, how excellent is Your name in all the earth. We give You thanks for this is the day that You have made, and we are rejoicing for we are glad in it! We magnify Your name, and we exalt You for You are the mighty and amazing God of all creation. Thank You, Lord, for the blessings and benefits of this day in Christ and for being in the land of all of Your creation.

We ask You Father for Your divine protection and safety from all that is hurtful and harmful to us. Keep us safe from every force of darkness and evil that the enemy tries to bring upon us. We give You thanks for the strong right hand of mercy that shields us from the dangers of life and the world that we live in. We rejoice in knowing that You are always our present help and that You provide a hedge of protection around us. Thank You for all the times that You send the angelic host to accompany us to allow our safe arrival at our destinations.

Lord, we ask that You allow the precious and powerful Blood of Jesus to cover us and every mode of transportation that we travel in. Lord, we ask that Your powerful, life-giving, lifesaving, and sanctifying Word will cover us and keep us. We ask Father that as we travel to and fro to accomplish Your will as Kingdom representatives and Kingdom ambassadors in the earth, You will not allow the enemy to prey upon or attack us or our loved ones. We rejoice in knowing that You are our refuge and strong tower; You are our shield and our protector in the time of need and in the time of trouble. Continue to remind us, Lord, that You are our way of escape from the storms of life that attempt to destroy us and overpower us.

Lord if You provided a pillar of fire for the Israelites by night and a cloud by day to lead Your people out of bondage, surely You can be our shield, our protector, our way maker, our highway through every wilderness season. We are grateful Lord that in our times of distress and darkness that You keep Your strong arms of protection around us. Thank You, Lord, for protecting us from the destructive force of evil and from the plots that satan plans for us.

Lord, we ask that no matter the strength or duration of the attacks that You will keep us covered under Your wings of protection. Your precious Blood keeps us and covers us so that the enemy's ways of evil, sin, and darkness cannot cross the bloodline and penetrate Your shield of protection. Lord You cause us to fear no evil for You are the shepherd who goes with us and goes before us. You protect us from dangers seen and unseen. Thank You Lord that You have promised to be our present help, to be with us at all times, and to never leave us nor forsake us. Therefore, we have no reason to fear. Thank You, Lord, for the security that we find in You. We ask that You will continue to bless and keep us in the name of Jesus. Amen.

Psalm 8 & 118

Purpose

Father, we come in the name of Jesus, the name at which every knee shall bow, and every tongue confess, to say thank You for being the Lord of our lives. Hear our cries and be merciful to us for we stand in need of answered prayers. Remind us that You are our God and You have made us for Your purposes. You reign and rule so that Your will is accomplished in the earth. Lord You have predestined us to be Your children and to partake of Your goodness and Your mercy and Your manifold blessings. You created us to do Your will in the earth. We ask that You will continue to use us for Your glory. Help us to be Your hands and feet; instruments and vessels that fulfill Your purpose for our creation.

Lord create in us a stronger desire to be intentional about fulfilling our purpose. We ask that You would help us to commit our ways to Your ways and to align our wills with Yours. Mold us and shape us as clay under the wheel of the potter so that we do only what we have been designed, created, and purposed to do. Help us to be real in all that we do and relevant in our times and seasons to make the impact needed to be Your instruments that help transform lives. Help us, Lord, to be faithful to our calling in ministry and service. Lord, we ask that You will help us to be obedient to the Spirit of the true and living God when our flesh refuses to obey Your will or pursue the mission that You have ordained. Help us, Lord, to remain focused, and Holy Spirit directed and anointed to fulfill Kingdom purpose. Help us to never forget why You created us and called us to serve and honor You. Help us to be faithful and obedient to the will, ways, and Word of God.

Lord as we throw ourselves on the altar, may our flesh be consumed by the fires of consecration and sanctification. May our sacrifices to fulfill our purpose and obey Your will be pleasing in Your sight. Let us offer up the sacrifice of praise and obedience that is a sweet fragrance to Your nostrils. Lord help us to live our lives to the fullest, knowing that our lives and our purpose are rooted and grounded in You, our God, and our creator. Remind us that nothing is more important in life than pleasing You and serving You in all of our ways.

Let us be purpose minded and purpose directed as we submit our lives for Your glory and for Your honor. Father, we ask for Your help in letting nothing, and no one interfere with the purposes that You have ordained for our lives. Let serving You and pleasing You in all our ways be our first priority as we acknowledge You for guidance and direction. Help us to be committed to a lifestyle of purposeful living. It is unto You Lord that we give thanks for helping us to find our purpose and for giving our lives meaning and significance. Let all that You have taught us about purpose be forever seared and emblazoned in our hearts and in our minds. We ask that You would transform and conform our lives daily for Your purposes. We give You thanks for saving us and choosing us not because of our works, but according to Your own purpose and plans. Father, we are forever grateful for all that You have done and we give You thanks in the name of Jesus. Amen.

Philippians 2, Jeremiah 18 & 29, II Timothy 1

God's Will

Father, it is in the name of Jesus, our Lord and our Savior that we humbly enter into Your presence. Thank You for the privilege to come freely and boldly before Your throne of grace. You are truly a merciful God, and we are forever grateful that You have given us the privilege and gift of prayer. We are thankful that Your will for our lives pervades in the earth. It was in Your prayer to the Father that You asked for His will to be done on earth and in heaven. Lord it is Your desire that man should forsake his evil, selfish, and fleshly ways to live a life surrendered to Your will. Let our will be surrendered and submitted to Your hands of grace and mercy.

We ask Father that You will let all that You have declared, decreed, and ordained for this world, this land, this country, this state, this city, our churches, and our lives come to pass as You have spoken. Remind us that whoever does the will of God, You call them members of Your family. Help us to be true worshippers as we strive to do Your will so that You will hear and answer our prayers and petitions.

When our flesh desires to control and lead us in the wrong direction, Lord let Your Holy Spirit rule and guide every thought and every action. Father, we ask that You would help us never to be conformed to the world or its ways and its evils, but to be transformed in our hearts and minds so that seeking Your will becomes good and acceptable for us. We ask You, Father, to let Your will dominate our thinking, our wills, our attitudes, and our behaviors. Let the ways of man take a backseat to every God ordained priority that aligns with Your Word, Your will, and Your ways.

Father, it is Your will that none should be lost or to perish, so Lord help us to make winning souls for the Kingdom to be our top priority. Help us to acknowledge You in all of our ways so that You will direct our paths according to Your will. Align our hearts and our minds with You Lord so that Your will takes pre-eminence in our lives.

Remind us, Lord, when we get caught up in ourselves that Your will abides forever; Your will is forever settled in heaven. Help us to live according to Your will and Your desires for us to live holy, upright before You and to keep Your commandments and obey Your Word.

Obedience to Your Word will help us to live fruitful and productive lives; blessed and prosperous lives. We ask for Your help Lord in sanctifying, consecrating our lives and to be holy in all our ways. Let our desire be to observe and do all that You require. We ask for Your help to live in fear and reverence of You. Then, Father, we ask in the name of Jesus that You will help us to fulfill Your will and purposes for our lives and to serve You faithfully for as long as we remain upon the earth.

It is in the mighty and matchless name of Jesus that we pray and ask these blessings. Amen.

Hebrews 4, Matthew 6, Mark 3, Psalm 119, II Peter 3

Healing

Father, we come in the name of Your Son Jesus, our Lord, and our Savior who died for the healing of the land and the healing of our bodies. We give You thanks for You have allowed us to know that whatever we ask in prayer, believing that we have received it, we know that it will be ours. We come in Your name, Jesus, knowing that if we cry out to You, we will be healed from all manner of sickness and disease, all manner of physical, emotional, and mental hurt. Lord, You remind us in Your Word that You are the one who heals us. You have healing powers that can cleanse us from all infirmities and impurities in our bodies, minds, souls, and spirits.

Gracious God You can even heal the brokenhearted, and You apply the balm of Gilead to comfort us in our brokenness and wounded states. Lord if You heal us, we will truly be healed. Thank You, Jesus, for carrying our sins and sickness on Your body and for hanging on the cross so that we could have more abundant lives. We ask that You remind us always of the lengths that You went to insure our healing and salvation. You were whipped and beaten beyond recognition. Precious and life-giving blood streamed from Your body because of the 39 stripes that You took for the healing of every disease. Thank You Lord for giving Your life for our healing and our well-being. You personally carried our sins and sickness in Your body so that our souls and our bodies could prosper and be in good health. Thank You, Lord, that because of Your completed work on the cross we can believe on Your word, stand on Your Word, and decree total healing for our minds and our bodies. The blood that You shed ensures deliverance from the infirmities that attempt to plague our bodies.

Father, we ask that You help us in the areas where our faith is too weak to believe for our healing. In Your name Jesus, we ask for healing over every cell, every tissue, every organ, every muscle, every nerve and every system within our bodies. Lord, we ask that You keep us in good health and that You speak to those areas of our bodies that are plagued by pain and sickness. We cry out to You Lord in our times of weakness and distress, asking You Lord to touch our bodies and speak a Word of deliverance from the ailments that torment us. Lord show us compassion and lay Your healing hands upon us, and we shall be made whole. We trust You and believe You Lord for that which we have prayed. Thank You for hearing our prayers and healing our bodies in Jesus' name. To You be all glory, and honor and praise. Amen and amen.

Isaiah 53, Mark 11, III John 1, Galatians 2, I Peter 2

Warfare

- Word and given us the whole armor to suit up for battle with. It is with our armor that we become armed and dangerous, suited for battle against the devil and his demonic spirits.

Lord, we ask that You would fight against those who fight against us and those who try to hinder our work with all manner of evil and criticism. Let their works be destroyed by their own negativity and critical spirits. Let embarrassment come upon them and shut their mouths, except for them to pray. Cover us from ambush and attack and help us to maintain faith under fire. Let us not be guilty of friendly fire upon fellow members of the Body of Christ.

Anoint us afresh for battle so that we can be battle ready and be victorious in defeat over the forces of darkness. Send the angelic host to accompany us and let us not be war casualties of the enemy. We thank You for victory in Jesus and for the power and authority that Jesus gave through His completed work on the cross. Thank You, Lord, for making us strong and courageous in spiritual warfare so that the works of the enemy never prevail over our lives.

Having done all Lord, we will gird our loins with truth. We will put on the breastplate of righteousness; we shod our feet with the gospel of peace. Lord, we ask that You will strengthen us so that we can take up the shield of faith and the helmet of salvation. Show us how to use the sword of the Spirit so that we can cut asunder the works of the enemy through believing the strong and powerful Word of the Most High God. We thank You for being our righteous redeemer and deliverer. May we ever hold fast to the truth of Your Word so that we can remain strong against every evil word and work of the enemy. We declare victory in Your name for every battle won, for we are more than conquerors because of the finished work on the cross. We thank You and we praise You in the name of Jesus we pray. Amen

Exodus 14, II Chronicles 20, Isaiah 54, Ephesians 6 & 12 , James 4, Luke 22

Mrs. Dana P. Richardson

Psalm 1:2-3 (NIV)
... but whose delight is in the law of the LORD,
and who meditates on his law day and night.
That person is like a tree planted by streams of water,
which yields its fruit in season
and whose leaf does not wither —
whatever they do prospers.

Ms. Dana Richardson is currently a Certified Lay Servant at Stewart Chapel United Methodist Church, where she serves the Lord through leading praise and worship, leads in worship, preaches, and teaches the

Word of God. Dana is Chairperson of Witness Ministries, where she operates in the prophetic, encourages our congregation and community, and anyone she meets. She is a prayer warrior, a playwright, and participates in creative arts ministry. Dana has been involved in creative writing and theatrical expressions since her teens. Her ministry is biblically based, and Holy Spirit led and inspired.

Inspiration

My late parents, Rev. Dr. Samuel J. Price, Sr., and Mrs. Rebecca F. Price are the "wind beneath my wings." Their parental guidance truly is my inspiration for everything I do. Prayer is the foundation of my existence as the youngest of five children. Praise, poetry, and plays keep me grounded in my faith-walk, and I want to share some of my innermost prayers with those who need a lift or light on this journey.

Ever-Present Help

Lord, You are an ever-present Help in our every time of need. You are always there, shining Your light in our darkness. Even when we cannot see our way, Your unfailing Love captures our attention. It serves as a constant reminder that You are a way maker. No one can make a way like You do. No one can calm a storm like You do. No one can lift a burden like You do. No one knows Your way, but we all know that You are the Way!

I love the way You reassure us that Your plans for us are greater and never will cause us harm. We may experience pain, suffering, or even times when we feel lonely, but Your presence is everywhere. Even when we feel left out, left behind or have taken a left turn, You always extend Your hands of mercy and provide us with Grace through Your Holy Spirit that guides us into all truths.

Forgive us for those times we overlook You, and those times we went to everyone without acknowledging You first. Lord, we know that You will not fail, that You cannot leave us alone, and that You will always be our ever-present Help! Thank You, Lord for holding us close, Dear God!

Thank You for leading us to Your place of peace when our mind wanders on our different paths of life. We are so thankful that You are able to allow rest in

Your Promise and provide comfort, strength, joy, and security when we need it most. In Jesus' name, we pray. Amen.

Calm My Fears

Lord, never in my life have I ever thought I would feel this way. Imagine me asking You such questions as "What's going on?" and "Don't You see what's happening?" or even "Where are You, Lord?" I am always wondering what next without considering that You are the same God that has rescued me before and will always be the same God to do it again. Yet, why am I scared to take the next step? Why am I afraid of what's coming next? I say that I trust You, and I believe it in my heart and mind, but my eyes are seeing it differently.

I keep repeating Psalm 23 and know that You are my Shepherd, dear Lord. I need to be comforted, and my mind needs to be at ease. My heart needs to feel Your presence, and I am waiting on You, Lord, to calm my fears. I am on my knees, with tears as my voice, dear Jesus. Please hold me near because I feel fear, I feel discomfort, and I feel pain. Lord, please help me understand that You are with me, and will never put more on me than I can bear, so I trust You and Your timing. I am asking You to once again hear my cry of help to calm my fears as I face _____(insert person, place or thing), knowing that You are always able and available to cast my anxieties away. Bring peace to my confused mind, and lift me with Your Word of hope and healing, above all that cause me any fear this day. In Jesus' name, Amen.

This one's personal!

Dear Lord, oh Jesus, You are my everything. You have proven Your love for me over and over again. You have shown me favor, You have given me more than I've ever hoped for, asked, or imagined.

Now, I need You, Lord, to meet a special need, to lend Your ear to an immediate request, and to answer swiftly as I call on Your powerful name. This time it's personal! Not for selfish gain, or impure motives, my God, I just need You to hear me. I need You to help me, and I need You to heal me because You said to ask, and it will be given, so I am standing, praying, fasting, expecting and trusting that You will be an on-time God!

Please Lord, God, I call forth a personal touch, a personal embrace and a personal release of Your Power because I'm grateful for Your steadfast Love shown toward me and I'm in need of Your constant care. Lord, please don't delay because I need You now, right now, and it's personal! In Jesus' name, Amen.

Dearly Beloved, We Gather Together

Lord, as I reflect on the start of wedding vows that so many couples have made and promised, Father God, I can't help but reflect on our first vow to You. I know we've made a vow to keep believing and serving You, Lord. Lord, teach us how to live and love as the first day we recited our vows to each other, as we have also made this commitment to You, dear God.

Remind us of our roles that we play and the patience, understanding, and wisdom that only You can give couples to have and to hold. Having little or having plenty means we work together to share our blessings with each other and bless those around us that we hold dear to our hearts. In sickness, let us be sensitive to the needs of our spouses, and in health, let us never grow weary in doing good physically, mentally, emotionally, socially, financially and more importantly, spiritually. Lord, let us always make time to be an Ecclesiastes 3 couple when choosing how and when we spend time together.

Time is something we cannot get back, so always lead us and guide us Lord through our decisions. Let us take each step by step to love and to cherish. Dear Lord, help us to bring You our plans so we may succeed, knowing everything operates in Your perfect timing and order. Help us, Father God, to build a strong foundation of trust and honesty, sharing our weaknesses and secrets, and relying on each other's' strengths. As we gather together, Lord, let us recognize that we are ministering as life partners, knowing our steps are ordered, our days are numbered, and our blessings are ordained by God.

Forgive us when we speak out of turn, step ahead of Your plans without acknowledging You first, or even times You need us to step aside, dear Jesus. Lord, I thank You for my marriage, my spouse, and my home. Fill our hearts, with love, igniting the passion we've had since date one. Keep us prayerful, cheerful, and thankful for each other, in the vows we forever live, until we are separated by death. In Jesus' name, Amen.

Breath Prayer

Lord, I come to You, not asking for anything. I come to You with thanksgiving for the air I breathe. As I breathe in, I take in the wonderful blessing of life. I realize that You are my Life! As I breathe out, I exhale that You are my Sustainer. I am able to live out the desires of my heart because You are my Keeper.

Dear Jesus, I just want to say thank You for every breath that You give. In Jesus' name, Amen

Help My Unbelief!

Father God, in the name of Jesus, I ask You right now to make me a believer again. I've witnessed what You've done in my life before and can't help but tell thank You for all You've done. Help me to see Your vision when my eyes are blurred. Help me to know that You have a far and better plan for my life. Right now, there are clouds of doubt and waves of disappointments that are bringing feelings of despair and disbelief.

I don't want to waver in my faith, so I am coming to You, Lord Jesus, asking humbly that You help my unbelief! Father, God, change my way of thinking and let me think on things that are pure and noteworthy. Lord, I have seen Your works, and I've witnessed what You've done for others. I know that You are able to do anything for anyone, so I need You to do this for me! I am sorry for feeling the way I do, but yet You know I'm human.

I know You love me and care so much for me, so please make me a believer of Your Word again. I ask that You show me Your marvelous works one more time, so I can believe again. In Jesus' name, Amen.

When Joy Comes

Father of Peace and Comfort, we know You give us Your Daily Bread. Your Word is our guiding light and provides life to us today. Your Word is our hope and helps us expect greater things to come tomorrow. We know Your Word will always stand. I am asking You, Dear God, to wipe tears of those in sadness and sorrow. I am asking You, Father, to strengthen the weak and the weary. God, I come to You, calling on and trusting Your Son, Jesus, who promised us a Comforter, The Holy Spirit, in our darkest hour and in our dry Season.

Someone's mourning, someone's lonely, and someone's in need of Your presence in their lives today, so please bring joy to their spirit, bring comfort to their soul and bring peace to their mind. We are thankful for Your presence in the midst of our storms, so please let us feel Joy again. We will be so grateful when Joy comes. In Jesus' name, Amen.

While Others Are Calling

Lord, I can call on Your name, Jesus, and know that I get Your attention. Whether morning, noon or night, I can trust that You will meet all of my needs. So many needs and so many names, yet while others are calling, You hear my voice. You know me well. You rescue me. You provide for me. For that, I just want to say thank You and know that while others are calling, bless them too, for You are a God who knows it all and provides for all of Your children.

Remember my prayer, dear Jesus, while others are calling on Your name, please don't forget about me. In Jesus' name, Amen.

Lord, Lift Me!

Lord, it has been one thing after another. Yet, I'm reminded that trouble we will have in this world always. I'm thankful that trouble doesn't last always. I choose to respond to trouble by coming to You in prayer. Lord, only You are able to lift me above what my eyes can see. I am looking to You, as my Helper and my Guide. Only You, dear God, can lift me beyond the circumstances that are in my path.

Dear Lord, only You can lift me to a place higher than I. I am so glad that You can see past my hurts, and understand my body language while in pain. I know by faith, You are working behind the scenes, and Your hands are moving mightily, working all things out for me. I can feel Your hand lifting me close, guiding me further down the journey and reaching out to see about me. I thank You, Lord, for always being there to lift me up when otherwise I would fall down. In Jesus' name, Amen.

Lord, Prepare Me

Lord, prepare me for what's to come, even though I may find it hard to handle or difficult to understand. Help me to ask for wisdom and guide me with Your Hand. For if You are preparing it for me, then there is a better plan bigger than what I can see right now. I know You've paced the best care into the works of whatever it is that You're preparing me for.

Lord, Jesus, please prepare me even though I'm afraid, I know You'll never leave me alone. You promised to keep watch over me, and that is in everything I do and say that brings You Glory.

I am asking You to keep a hedge of protection around me. Remind me that You have commanded angels to have charge over my life. Lord, prepare me for whatever comes what may and accept what You allow in my life. For I know my life is in Your hands. Lord, prepare my heart, my mind, my soul, and my spirit for whatever it is, for I know that You know what's best and have already prepared it. In Jesus' name, Amen.

Mrs. Sherri Pinckney Kinloch

Philippians 4:10-13
I rejoiced in the Lord greatly that now at length you have revived your concern for me. You were indeed concerned for me, but you had no opportunity. Not that I am speaking of being in need, for I have learned in whatever situation I am to be content. I know how to be brought low, and I know how to abound. In any and every circumstance, I have learned the secret of facing plenty and hunger, abundance and need. I can do all things through him who strengthens me.

Mrs. Sherri Pinckney Kinloch. I endured many hardships in life, like so many others have, of course, but during one of the darkest hours of my life, God spoke to me through a verse of scripture found in Joel 2:25-26 that says, "And I will restore to you the years that the locust hath eaten, the cankerworm, and the caterpillar, and the palmerworm, my great army which I sent among you. And ye shall eat in plenty, and be satisfied, and praise the name of the Lord your God, that hath dealt wondrously with you: and my people shall never be ashamed." God promised me greater for all of the suffering that I endured and He promised me that I would never experience the shame of my past ever again. My God is so faithful!

As a young child, I was sexually assaulted and bullied, and I was a victim of a date rape at the age of sixteen. I was a broken mess!! I never expected to be a teen mother, but just a few years later, I received one of the greatest gifts I have ever received. I became a mother at the age of 19 to my beautiful, baby boy, Rashad. Many personal struggles followed, and I endured many disappointments in my personal life that destroyed my self-esteem, and for many years I didn't love myself at all. My lack of self-love led me into unhealthy relationships where I suffered years of physical and emotional abuse at the hands of people who claimed to love me.

I didn't know it then, and I didn't understand why God would allow me to experience so much pain. Was I a horrible person that God was punishing or did He just forget about me? Neither of these things were true, but the enemy knew exactly what he was doing. The enemy came to destroy me, but God had a purpose for my pain. He spoke to my heart and let me know that every tear that I shed, and every sleepless night, and every struggle that I endured, was necessary for Him to make me into the strong woman of God that I am today. My life is a living testimony! Someone is going through a difficult time, and they've lost faith in themselves, lost faith in their family, and lost faith in God's love for them. He is using me as a vessel to pour into you what He has poured into to me, to give you hope for tomorrow. A brighter day is coming! You may be weeping right now, but joy is on the way! (Psalms 30:5)

In the midst of my struggles, God allowed me (after eight years of going to school at night, while working a full-time and part-time job, and being a single mother) to be the first person, in my immediate family, to graduate from college. Through the encouragement, love, and support of my parents, I was able to obtain a Bachelor of Science in Business Management degree at the age of 35. I have been blessed to have a great career in Property and Project Management for the past 18 years, and He has blessed me to finally have the love that I always wanted and needed with my husband, Derrick.

Inspiration

God made me a promise in 2014, and all I had to do was to trust Him and be obedient. I did, and He has given me double for my troubles! He restored everything that I lost with more than I had before, He gave me a love that I have never had, and He has allowed me to make peace with my past. So, I can say this with joy and confidence. I know that my God is faithful "...forgetting those things which are behind and reaching forth unto those things which are before. I press toward the mark for the prize of the high calling of God in Christ Jesus" (Philippians 3:13-14), and because I know who I am in Him I give Him all praises for the good, the bad and the ugly because He worked it out for my good!!

The prayers that I've written came through quiet meditation and reflection on the goodness of my God, and all that He has brought me through. Nothing can separate me from His love!!

May God bless you as you read these prayers and may the words that you read inspire you, captivate you, and bless your soul.

God bless!

Strength

Mighty God, in whom I look to for strength and protection. Blessing, glory, and honor all belong to You.

I ask that as I begin my journey today in this thing called life, that You shield, cover, and protect me from the hands of the enemy.

I ask that You would allow Your angels to surround me, and protect me from seen and unseen dangers, plots, schemes, and plans that the enemy has devised for my destruction.

I ask that You show up in this situation and cause my enemies to fall at my feet, cause those things that were meant to destroy me to bless me, cause those things that were meant to defeat me to be defeated.

I know that as Your child, that if I ask anything in Your name, it shall be done, so I declare that victory is mine, I declare that no weapon formed against me shall prosper, and I declare that this prayer will be heard and answered in the name of Jesus! Amen.

Gratefulness

Compassionate God, I come to You today with a grateful heart full of praise for You and how You constantly and consistently shower me with Your love.

Even when I fall short in doing or saying the things I should, You are still faithful to me.

Thank You for never giving up on me, and for gently leading me with Your love, and tender guidance.

Allow Your light to shine in and through my life, so that others may be able to see it and desire to know the God that I love and serve for themselves.

Let there be a word, deed, or action that comes forth from me that will be a blessing to someone today.

I declare this to be done in the name of Jesus! Amen.

Healing

Oh, Father God, I thank You for allowing me to see another day. I'm thankful to You, God, because the doctor's report was not the final report. I thank You, oh God, for touching me with Your finger of love, for healing my body, dear Father, again and again. I thank You for removing the sickness and disease from my body. I thank You for total and complete healing in the name of Jesus.

I asked, dear God, that You continue to pour out Your blood that it may cleanse me of all unrighteousness and iniquities, and that it may make me whole just as You did with the woman with the issue of blood. I know that a touch from You will bring forth healing dear God, so I thank You in advance for my healing.

I thank You for how You've prepared the physicians and the nurses and everyone that will participate in my healing. I thank You, God, for how You're going to use them, Holy Father to bless me. I declare and decree this to be so in Jesus' name, Amen!!

Mercy

Merciful God, full of compassion, love, and grace, I'm thankful for how You have allowed me to see another glorious day that You have created. The sunlight shown on my face, I awakened refreshed and renewed and I slept peacefully through the night in a comfortable bed. I know that it is only because of Your love that I had a place to lay my head, food to eat, and shelter from the dangers of this world. I can't give You enough praise for all of the many things that You do for me, my family, and loved ones.

I never want to forget those that are less fortunate than I am. I know that You see them and know them all by name, so I ask dear God for an extra portion of love, compassion, grace, and deliverance upon my brother or my sister that for reasons that are unknown to me, have found themselves in situations that they can't find their way out of.

Touch their hearts, my Master, draw them nearer, so that they will come running towards You and they can begin life anew. Speak to their hearts so that a word, deed, or action would touch them in a special way and in that moment they would feel Your presence.

I thank You for the souls that will be delivered, and the blessings that will come from faith and obedience to Your Word. I thank You, I praise You, and I exalt You! In the name of Jesus, Amen.

Marriage

Holy Father, we know that there is power in unity. The enemy knows that if he can divide us, he can destroy us. When a man and woman come together as one in Holy Matrimony, the power that they possess is multiplied. You're not a threat to the enemy when You indulge in premarital sex or others actions that God ordained for a man and his wife, but when You decide to become one, it destroys the enemies plan for Your destruction.

My prayer, oh God, is that You would allow this marriage bond to be built on a foundation of love for You, love, honor, respect and loyalty to each other and be overflowing with compassion and understanding. We commit ourselves totally and completely to You, so that You may be glorified through this marriage. Let others see this union and desire to have the same relationship or better with their spouses.

We know that there will be disagreements, but let those disagreements be resolved peacefully and respectfully. You said in Your Word that *a man that findeth a wife finds a good thing*; so, let that same joy that he felt when he found her continue to shower blessings upon their union. We declare and decree a marriage filled with love and longevity. In the name of Jesus, Amen.

Be Steadfast

Dear Lord, when my enemies and those that say that they love me, allow satan to use them, help me to lean on Your Word and be reminded that You are "...not deceived;...for whatsoever a man soweth that shall he also reap. For he that soweth to his flesh shall of the flesh reap corruption, but he that soweth to the Spirit shall of the Spirit reap life everlasting." Strengthen me so that I will "....not be weary in well-doing", and trust You and know that Your promises are true and that if I hold on and wait on you, in due season, I will reap if I faint not." (Gal 6:7-9).

In other words, my breakthrough is on the way. My deliverance is on the way. I'm about to walk into the purpose and the promise that You prepared just for me. So, keep me humbled God.

Let me be steadfast, unmovable and always abounding in the Word of the Lord. Don't let my labor be in vain, don't let my suffering and my heartache be in vain, don't let my enemies rejoice over me. In the name of Jesus, I pray, Amen.

Hope

Blessings, glory, and honor all belong to You and only You, oh Lord, my help, my strength, and my redeemer. It's in the lowest places in my life that I find safety in Your arms. You are my rock, my deliverer and my peace. When I had given up on myself and couldn't see a brighter day ahead, You reminded me that I am fearfully and wonderfully made. You reminded me that because I am Your child, that there isn't anything good that You will withhold from me.

You reminded me that I shouldn't grow weary in well-doing, because if I kept on believing, kept on trusting, and held on just a little while longer, that I would have wings like an eagle and be able to soar above the negativity, heartbreak, depression, and anxiety in my life.

You give me hope for tomorrow, and each day that I have life, I'm going to praise You, honor You, and magnify Your Holy and righteous name. Thank You for Your love. In the name of Jesus, I pray, Amen.

Honor

Almighty God, my deliverer, and my protector. "Have mercy upon me, on God, according to Your lovingkindness, According to the multitude of Your tender mercies, blot out my transgressions, wash me thoroughly from my iniquity and cleanse me from my sin." (Psalms 51:1-2).

Heavenly Father, when I call on You, You answer. When I need You, You are always there. You are sovereign, merciful, and worthy of all of my praise. There is not a need that You haven't met, there is not a problem that You haven't solved, and there's no one in my life that loves me like You do. You've seen me at my best and at my worse, and You never turned away from me.

You kept on loving me through my periods of disobedience. You loved me when I fell short and waited for me to return to You, and I'm so grateful for the opportunity to say I'm Your child and You are my Heavenly Father. I will bless Your name, forevermore. In Jesus' name, Amen.

Glory

"Bless the Lord, O my soul: and all that is within me, bless his holy name." (Psalm 103:1) God of Heaven and of Earth. My Alpha and my Omega. My help in troubling times. You've allowed the plans of my enemies to fail. You've allowed me to prosper in the midst of turmoil in my life, You've caused my enemies wicked plans to work for my good, You've caused my enemies to bless me and left them confused.

When I reflect on just how good, how GREAT, and how awesome You are, I can't stop giving You glory, honor, and praise. I will forever bless Your name. Thank You for life, health and strength. Thank You for blessing me beyond measure. Thank You for answered and unanswered prayers.

Thank You for smoothing out the rough edges of my life and making my crooked paths straight. Thank You for just being God Almighty! In the name of Jesus, I pray, Amen.

Praise

"Great is Thy faithfulness," O God my Father, There is no shadow of turning with Thee; Thou changest not, Thy compassions, they fail not As Thou hast been Thou forever wilt be." (Song by Chris Rice, written By Thomas O. Chisolm.) Your love never waivers, Your love never fails.

Your love for me awakens my spirit daily and causes my soul to desire more of You. To know more, to fellowship with You more, to love You more.

My heart leaps for joy at the very mention of Your name. My excitement can't be constrained when I think of where You've brought me from, and what You've brought me out of.

I can't help but lift my voice and shout hallelujah to the Most High God. You promised in Your word that "When thou passest through the waters, I will be with thee; and through the rivers, they shall not overflow thee: when thou walkest through the fire, thou shalt not be burned; neither shall the flame kindle upon thee." (Isaiah 43:2)

I will continue to lift up Your name, to exalt You, and worship You my God. Nothing I have exists without You, nothing I do is without You, and I will reverence You all the days of my life. In the name of Jesus, Amen.

Scripture and Song References

Cleveland, James 1980, *Peace Be Still*. p.56

Crosby, Fanny 1873, *Blessed Assurance*. p.57

James 5:16 (KJV) "The effectual fervent prayer of the righteousness man availeth much." p.65

Dorsey, Thomas A., 1943- *The Lord Will Make A Way Somehow*. p.71

Isaiah 54:17 (KJV) No weapon that is formed against thee shall prosper; and every tongue that shall rise against thee in judgment thou shalt condemn. This is the heritage of the servants of the LORD, and their righteousness is of me, saith the LORD. pp. 71, 79

1 Peter 2:9 (NIV) tells me that I am a chosen people, a royal priesthood, a holy nation, Gods possession, that I may declare the praises of him who called me out of darkness into His wonderful light. p.75